W9-DCE-214

Joan L. Roccasalvo, C.S.J.

THE IGNATIAN INFLUENCE ON THE SPIRITUALITY OF THE SISTERS OF ST. JOSEPH

Congregation of St. Joseph
Brentwood, NY 11717
and
Montrose Publishing Company
Montrose PA 18801

1993

Congregation of St. Joseph Brentwood, NY
The Montrose Publishing Company

Copyright © 1993 by Joan L. Roccasalvo, C.S.J.

ISBN: 0-9638407-0-3

Cover Design and Illustrations by Marion C. Honors, C.S.J.

THE IGNATIAN INFLUENCE ON

THE SPIRITUALITY

OF

THE SISTERS OF ST. JOSEPH

This book is dedicated
to all Sisters of St. Joseph
and to their Associate Members
serving the neighbor
to build up the Body of Christ.

CONTENTS

PREFACE

The seeds of this work were planted in 1970 when I requested an exclaustration from the Brentwood province of the Sisters of St. Joseph. Two years later, after doing the *Spiritual Exercises* of St. Ignatius, I renewed my commitment to the Lord Jesus as a Sister of St. Joseph.

Since 1972, I have studied the *Maxims of Perfection* together with the *Spiritual Exercises*. These Ignatian *Exercises* are the matrix and full expression of the *Maxims of Perfection*, "which contain the entire spirit of the Sisters of St. Joseph."[1] Through the *Maxims*, Fr. Médaille envisions God's loving design "for all aspiring to great virtue"[2] according to the apostolic spirituality which had formed his own life as a Jesuit.

I would like to share the fruits of my study and prayer with my sisters in Christ in the hope that they will derive benefit for themselves and for those whom they serve. A special thanks to my artist-friend Marion C. Honors, C.S.J. for her friendship and especially for her presence during my spiritual odyssey in Florence, Italy. She has provided not only the cover and illustrations for this book but also many valuable suggestions. A special word of thanks must also go to Emily Joseph Daly, C.S.J., to Eileen Lomasney, C.S.J. and to those Sisters of St. Joseph wishing to go unnamed for their gracious collaboration on this work.

This work could not have been completed without the encouragement of Rosemary Barrett, C.S.J., Edyth T. Fitzsimmons, C.S.J., John Raymond McGann, C.S.J., Francis Teresa O'Reilly, C.S.J., Clara T. Santoro, C.S.J. and of George A. Aschenbrenner, S.J., John J. Begley, S.J., George E. Ganss, S.J., John J. Levko, S.J., Brian O'Leary, S.J., and Joseph P. Whelan, S.J.

The conciliar document, *Perfectae caritatis*, called for a revitalization of religious institutes of men and women through discovering or re-discovering the origins of their spiritual identity and to interpret their meaning in light of contemporary needs. Postconciliar studies on religious life have reiterated the decree of Vatican II. The most recent of these states that "a return to the spirit of the founder was identified as a critical part of this renewal process.[3] Sisters of St. Joseph are called to breathe new life into the spirit of the charism bequeathed to them by Jean-Pierre Médaille of the Society of Jesus. The spirit of the Sisters of St. Joseph is rooted in its proper and legitimate source--the *Spiritual Exercises*, the matrix of the *Maxims of Perfection*.

In 1989 the joint meeting of the Conference of Major Superiors of Men and the Leadership Conference of Women Religious meeting in Louisville, KY issued a statement listing ten transformative elements for religious life in the future. They are as follows:

1. Prophetic Witness: Being converted by the example of Jesus and the values of the gospel, religious in the year 2010 will serve a prophetic role in church and society. Living this prophetic witness will include critiquing societal and ecclesial values and structures, calling for systemic change and being converted by the marginalized with whom we serve.

2. Contemplative Attitude Toward Life: Religious in 2010 will have a contemplative attitude toward all creation and be motivated by the presence of the sacred.

3. Poor and Marginalized Persons as the Focus for Ministry: Religious in 2010 will be investing their resources in direct service with and advocacy for structural change on behalf of the poor and marginalized.

4. Spirituality of Wholeness and Global Interconnectedness: Animated by their deep conviction of the oneness of creation, religious in 2010 live and work in a manner which fosters:

a. participation and harmony among all people,
b. healthy personal and interpersonal relationships,
c. reverence for the earth,
d. integration of spirituality and technology on behalf of the gospel.

5. Charism and Mission as Sources of Identity: By the year 2010, religious groups will have re-examined, reclaimed and set free the charisms of their foundresses/founders.

6. Change of the Locus of Power: Religious in 2010 have replaced models of domination and control with principles of mutuality drawn from feminist and ecological insights, so that collaborative modes of decision-making and power-sharing are normative.

7. Living with Less: Religious in the year 2010 will be transformed by the poor, living a simpler life-style that includes reverence for the earth.

8. Broad-based, Inclusive Communities: In 2010 religious communities will be characterized by inclusivity and intentionality. They will have a core group and persons with temporary and permanent members.

9. Understanding Ourselves as Church: An essential element of religious life in 2010 is our ability to accept the concept that "we are church." As people of God, we assume our priestly role of shared leadership in the life and worship of the church. We support all members of the church as equals in diverse ministries.

10. Developing Interdependence Among People of Diverse Cultures: By the year 2010, radical demographic changes will alter the face of our local church and our congregations. Our interactions with persons of various cultures and races have uncovered our enduring racism, inculturation, interdependence and openness to being evangelized by others.

Fr. Médaille's teaching echoes that of his spiritual father, St. Ignatius of Loyola: like the Society of Jesus, the Sisters of St. Joseph are called to live as contemplatives in action. Theirs is a practical mysticism: union with God is to be found in the ordinary, performed with extraordinary reverence and beauty, with the most profound humility and the most cordial charity towards everyone whom they encounter.

To some readers, this book will seem incomplete because it lacks our complete story as Sisters of St. Joseph. The history of the Sisters of St. Joseph from the seventeenth century to the present is vast and varied, and it would be impossible to narrate in any systematic way the pointillistic details of this heritage. Others more qualified than I have spent years studying the history of the Congregation, province by province. Readers seeking additional information about the Sisters of St. Joseph may consult the bibliography in addition to the endnotes. I have narrowed my focus to the influence of the *Spiritual Exercises* on the *Maxims of Perfection*.

J.L.R.
8 September 1993

Perhaps you feel like the women on Easter morning?
At first downhearted:
The death of Jesus means the end of all their dreams. . .
Then, overjoyed, they recognize Him alive!

Now see how they hurry, those first women,
to spread the news!
They must tell everyone, they must shout aloud
what has happened, and what now gives them a reason to live.

This is what the Sisters of St. Joseph
wish to do with you, dear reader, and with all who believe
in Jesus' death and resurrection.

By a Sister of St. Joseph of the French Federation

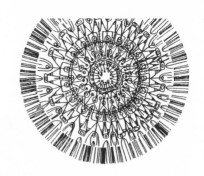

PART ONE

THE FOUNDER

As kingfishers catch fire, dragonflies dráw fláme

. . . The just man justices;
Kéeps gráce; thát keeps all his going graces;
Acts in God's eye what in God's eye he is--
Chríst--for Christ plays in ten thousand places,
Lovely in limbs, and lovely in eyes not his
To the Father through the features of men's faces.[4]

Gerard Manley Hopkins

JEAN-PIERRE MEDAILLE, S.J.

ON OCTOBER 6, 1610 JEAN-PIERRE MÉDAILLE WAS BORN TO JEAN Médaille, the king's counselor and to Philippe d'Estevenel in the French medieval city of Carcassonne. Jean-Pierre attended the *collège* there conducted by the Society of Jesus. In 1626 he entered the Jesuit novitiate at Toulouse and was ordained in 1637. His younger brother Jean-Paul also became a Jesuit priest.[6] Two future saints lived contemporaneously with Jean-Pierre-- Saints John Francis Régis (1609-1652) and Noël Chabanal (1613- 1649), the latter numbering among the seven North American Jesuits martyred in Canada in 1649. The careers of Jean-Pierre and John Francis Régis included the same kinds of ministry: home mission work and educational and social work within the Toulouse province.[7]

In *A History of the Society of Jesus*, William Bangert attributes the founding of the Sisters of St. Joseph to the younger Médaille, Jean-Paul, instead of to Jean-Pierre.[8]

Fr. Jean-Pierre Médaille served as teacher, minister, procurator, preacher and spiritual director at the following *collèges*:

Carcassone	1633-1635
Montauben	1642-1643
Saint Flour	1643-1649
Aurillac	1650-1654
Montiferrand	1654-1662
Clermont	1662-1669
Billom	1669[9]

While serving at Saint Flour, Fr. Médaille preached a mission in Le Puy.[10] In 1650, the Bishop of Le Puy, Henri de Maupas received the fledgling group and officially recognized the "Little Design" of women needed to serve in Le Puy. The first six sisters, Francoise Eyraud, Clauda Chastel, Marguerite Burdier, Anna Chaleyer, Anna Vey and Anna Braun, embraced the ascetical teaching and practice lived by their founder.

The records tell us very little about Fr. Médaille. Frail in health, his temperament is described as "good and peaceloving, melancholy, bilious and balanced, and his intelligence as "excellent, remarkable, penetrating and sublime [with] "an aptitude for all the works of the Society."[11] Some said that "he was born for the missions;" still others spoke of "his great aptitude for the instruction and direction of souls.[12] Jean-Pierre Médaille excelled in matters practical, intellectual and spiritual. In short, he was a man of great versatility. The founder of the Sisters of St. Joseph died in 1669.

The necrology for Jean-Pierre Médaille reads as follows:

Father Jean-Pierre Médaille of Carcassonne, professed of four vows, died at Billom, 1669, at the age of fifty-nine. He had been in the Society for forty-three years. The greater part of his life was spent in the missions of the province (Toulouse) with such great zeal and so great a reputation for holiness that here and there he was called 'the saint,' 'the apostle.' Nor were the fruits of his apostolic labors of every kind less than his reputation, so much so that he was highly esteemed by rich and poor alike, but especially by the bishops in whose dioceses he labored.[13]

Jean-Pierre Médaille "reflects the breadth of service practiced by the Society [of Jesus] and evidently inherent in his own talents in the ministries and in the openness to ministry which he bequeathed to the Sisters of St. Joseph."[14]

PART TWO

FOUNDING

To Celebrate a Time

To celebrate a time, a sacred year,
was God's idea. In Leviticus
the word that came to Moses reads like this:
"Send someone out to blow the yôbel horn
of jubilee, announcing through the land
this year is sacred and is set apart
to make the great return, and to proclaim
freedom to every last inhabitant."
(FREEDOM written large, in his most holy Name,
for God was speaking from a Father's heart.)
And then he said: "And let the land lie fallow
all this year. Earth, too, has need of healing:
let it rest. Let time itself be hallowed.
Then celebrate my covenant with prayer
and praise, with dancing and sweet song . . .
and tell again the stories you have heard
about my providence through ages long."

The centuries pass: The Word Made Flesh has come.
A Life, a Death, a Resurrection tale
fulfills the covenant and shows the way
to build up Kingdom Come. The terms are difficult
in an expanding world. Time quickens to a hum

and history obscures the common day,
and all the courage that it takes
to live just one of them that seeks
no sign of human comfort in return . . .
just like that day in eighteen thirty-six
in Lyons, France. Oh, no apocalypse
of light: no voice from Sinai, but a sign--
(hand-lettered beautifully, of course), affixed
there on a convent wall where even
novices and postulants would see it
(and they did). The sign read: VOLUNTEERS
FOR THE AMERICAN MISSION. The ship
was sailing January fourth, and six
young women filled with love, and hope, and dreams
would be aboard. Imagine leaving home
at Christmas time: Epiphany at sea . . .
Oh, think of everything this means:
a cold Atlantic crossing, America so far!
"Les anges dans nos compagnes . . ." but no star
to guide them like the Magi. Only foam
and brine and motion, sickening motion
of wind and wave in an unfriendly ocean.
And why? Why take a risk at all in foreign lands?
For this: the need was there. They'd be his hands,
his feet, his loving heart for every child
of God they'd find--in any kind of need.
Something of fire burned in them . . . something of flame!
they'd keep the covenant for God in Jesus's name.

One hundred fifty years have passed since those
whose names are poetry to read stepped down
the gang-plank on the Mississippi shore.
The names have changed: the stories are the same--
with variations. But every story shows
with what munificence of grace a pattern grows . . .
as David in his psalm had sung before:
"His plan will stand forever. The design
of his heart through all the generations."
Yes, the names change, and the dear good faces,
and some go off to farther foreign places:
a carpenter for patron--and for sign?
The great love of our God: that love which binds
our human lives together across time.

This is the time we consecrate, return--
not perfect . . . flawed, but given as we can.
We celebrate it all this sacred year
with praise, and thank, according to your word.
We would be reconciled, Our Father, free
with that great freedom we have often heard
your own Son speak of--spirit-filled and true.
We would be lovers, Father, of your world with you.
Bless with new life those women who have gone,
and help us, with your grace, to face the dawn.[14]

Eileen Lomasney, C.S.J.

WHO ARE THE SISTERS OF ST. JOSEPH?

INTRODUCTION

THE SISTERS OF ST. JOSEPH WERE FOUNDED IN LE PUY, FRANCE, ca. 1650 under the direction of the Jesuit priest, Jean-Pierre Médaille.[16] At the time of his death in 1669, the "daughters of St. Joseph" were living the apostolic spirituality of the Society of Jesus founded by St. Ignatius of Loyola in 1540. Today approximately twenty-five thousand Sisters of St. Joseph serve in diverse ministries on every continent.[17] The *Spiritual Exercises* of St. Ignatius are the inspiration and source of Fr. Médaille's *Maxims of Perfection* which "contain the entire spirit of the Institute and of the Constitutions."[18] The *Maxims of Perfection* originate from the book of the *Spiritual Exercises*.

THE EARLY INSTITUTE OF ST. JOSEPH

The founding of the Sisters of St. Joseph was a bold and daring enterprise. These women met and prayed together and ministered without the traditional supports of the cloister or even of religious garb.[19] They dressed simply "adopt[ing] the clothes worn by widows in their locality, which varied from [region to region]."[20] The prevalence of war "meant that the widow's habit was the most common form of dress for a woman, so that a sister wearing it could walk freely about the streets on her apostolic work."[21]

The Sisters of St. Joseph are among the first congregations of women to labor outside the cloister. From their beginnings, they were engaged in a mobile apostolate extremely varied and adapted to local needs. They understood that because God is present and at work in all things, union with God was possible in their dealings with people and circumstances as well as in the experience of prayer.

The Daily Examen would become a spiritual exercise indispensable for reviewing one's efforts to find God in the humdrum happenings of daily life which combined contemplation and action. This prayer is a structural part of Ignatian spirituality. Its importance is highlighted in the *Spiritual Exercises* (#24-43) but also in the following two reflections, the first by St. Ignatius writing to scholastics engaged in studies, the second by Fr. Médaille in one of the maxims:

> "Consider the end of your studies. The scholastics can hardly give themselves to prolonged meditations. Over and above the spirtual exercises assigned for their perfection, namely daily Mass, an hour for vocal prayer and examen of conscience, weekly confession and communion, they should practice the seeking of God in all things, in their conversation, their walks, in all that they see, taste, hear, understand, in all their actions, since His Divine Majesty is truly in all things by His presence, power and essence . . . this method is an excellent exercises to prepare us for great visitations of our Lord.[22]

> "Desire the perfection suitable to the three powers of your soul: for the memory, a forgetfulness of all things, even of self, in order to remember God alone; for the seeing of God in all things, the glory, the power, the providence, the mercy of God; for the will, the liberty of approaching God, of loving God and of embracing all the orders of God's providence with all the affection of your soul."

The early Jesuits and later the Sisters of St. Joseph embraced an apostolate which directed their members to go anywhere and do whatever was needed to minister to others.

In addition to personal and liturgical prayer, the daily examen enabled active women to reflect on every aspect of their lives, physical, spiritual, material and mental in order to discern God's good pleasure.

Conditions in France during the sixteenth and seventeenth centuries were not too different in essence from the human condition today which may be characterized by a vacuum of spiritual values, greed and materialism, political unrest and social injustice.[23] Our first 'sisters' placed themselves at the disposal of the local Church and answered the call to serve in these conditions. How could this simple association of vowed lay women, though serving outside the cloister, foster a life of deep prayer?[24] The greatest spiritual maturity was needed for these women who would allow others to make demands on their time and energy, their patience and wisdom. Their inner life had to be strong and serene in order to bring that love emanating from their affective union with God to others.

As Jesus derived inner strength from those periods of solitary prayer with his Father, so too the Sisters of St. Joseph. For them, apostolic spirituality was nothing more than love in action, and it transformed them into affective and effective leaders of the seventeenth-century Church. This total gift of oneself to God is expressed in the "Suscipe" of St. Ignatius, first as found in the book of the *Exercises*, the second in the old Formulary of Prayers of the Sisters of St. Joseph:

> "Take, Lord, and receive all my liberty, my memory, my understanding, and all my will--all that I have and possess. You, Lord, have given all that to me. I now give it back to you, O Lord. All of it is yours. Dispose of it according to your will. Give me your love and your grace, for that is enough for me." (#234)

> "Receive, O my God, my liberty which I offer to Thee, without reserve; accept of my memory, understanding, and will all that I have, all that I am. Thou hast given all to me, I only return them to Thee that Thou mayest dispose of them according to Thy loving and amiable pleasure."

Before proceeding any further, a distinction should be made between the book and experience of the *Spiritual Exercises*. The book itself is the written record of St. Ignatius' experience of God which "sprang from the rich mystical experiences and the dynamic principles with which God gifted him."[25] It was refined during the course of his lifetime. With the Bible as the starting point, the book of the *Exercises* contains a set of guidelines for the director while guiding a retreatant. It is "not to be *read* so much as *prayed*, [and] a cursory reading is bound to lead to disappointment."[26]

The experience of the *Spiritual Exercises* may be described as a deep and prolonged experience of personal prayer. They embody various forms of prayer whose goal is interior freedom so that the whole of one's life will be lived at the faith level. The experience deepens one's awareness of God's overwhelming love which makes all things possible. Part Three will focus more closely on the book and experience of the *Spiritual Exercises* as they relate to the *Maxims of Perfection*.

A TRINITARIAN CHARISM

The charism of the Sisters of St. Joseph is rooted in that of St. Ignatius as lived by Father Médaille.[27] What is the meaning of the word 'charism'? A charism (Gr. *charis*) begins with an unmerited religious experience of depth and intensity. God singles out a particular individual and touches that person with an unforgettable experience of love in which s/he is given a special understanding of the Divine Mystery. In humility, the graced person is caught up in the triune God and is ready to respond as the Spirit beckons. John Futrell summarizes:

> "The mode of receiving the charism is shaped then, by the person's historical and cultural conditioning, as well as by his temperament, human gifts and limitations; all of which Christians recognize as the effects of God's active love in history."[28]

In the Judeo-Christian tradition, the names of Moses, St. Paul, St. Ignatius of Loyola, St. Teresa of Avila, our own Mother St. John Fontbonne and Mother Teresa are examples of highly graced individuals.

It was at Manresa near the River Cardoner that Ignatius received from God great illuminations into the mystery of the Holy Trinity and of God's energizing all of creation. Michael Ivens says that "the Trinity for Ignatius is emphatically the creator and redeemer God, continually at work in 'all things.'"[29] Of this pure unmerited gift Ignatius says unpretentiously: ". . . his [Ignatius'] understanding began to be elevated so that he saw the Holy Trinity in the form of three musical keys . . . [which] brought on so many tears and so much sobbing that he could not control himself."[30] In the solitude of Manresa, Ignatius could not have envisioned the profound impact that this mystical experience would have in leading him to found the Society of Jesus. Yet he allowed God to lead him gently toward this end.

Ignatius understood the Trinity as the real presence of Persons. For him and later for Fr. Médaille, to participate in the life of the Trinity was to be caught up in the paschal mystery of the Lord Jesus, Son of the Father through the power of the Spirit, and of our pilgrimage to spiritual freedom in God. When Ignatius conceptualized his understanding of the trinitarian mystery, he did so from the lived experience and not from abstract formulae. He came to see that "all creatures are related to God," a fact that "he came to experience directly for himself."[31] God is Pure Act, i.e., God is at work energizing all creation. This meant that Ignatius too was at work in the concrete situations of life. He handed on this practical spirituality to his Jesuit confreres and they to others. The following maxim conveys the largesse of the Ignatian spirit:

> "Embrace, at least in desire, the conversion and sanctification of the whole world in imitation of apostolic persons and do so with a generous courage which, in the orders of God's good pleasure and of obedience and in the observance of true humility, brings you and urges you to wish to do everything

and to suffer everything in order to glorify God, assist in the salvation and sanctification of those who cost God's dear Son everything."

Years later, Ignatius narrated that he seemed to see Christ with the cross on his shoulders and beside him the Eternal Father who said to him, "I wish you to take this man [Ignatius] as your servant, and Jesus so took him and said, "My will is that you should serve us." Thus Ignatius was to serve the Holy Trinity by taking the crucified Lord into the contemporary world. Hugo Rahner says that "this reveals the underlying structure of Ignatian theology--above, below and middle.[32] His comments are perfectly paralleled in Fr. Médaille's Consecration to the Two Trinities.[33] In the *Maxims*, Fr. Médaille speaks of the Holy Trinity and the trinity of the Holy Family. The following maxim exemplifies Fr. Médaille's trinitarian devotion:

> "Consecrate yourself often to the holy and uncreated Trinity of God, Father, Son and Holy Spirit. To the created one of Jesus, Mary and Joseph, and to all the saints of heaven."

In this divine descent, Ignatius found God 'above' which enabled him to find God 'below' in the contemporary world.[34] In between was "Christ the Mediator as incarnate God, the creator and Lord who had become a creature."[35] Centuries earlier the Eastern Fathers phrased this theology in what would become one of the best-loved verses of Eastern Christianity: "God became one of us that we might become as God."

The motto "for the greater glory of God" implies that Ignatius saw God as the beginning and end of that life which comes to us from Jesus through the Spirit. It was by being an intimate companion of Jesus that one entered into the life of the Trinity. This life was to be lived not in the cloister but in the world. The trinitarian charism of Ignatius of Loyola stands as the cornerstone in the spirituality of the Sisters of St. Joseph and many other religious congregations. The pre- and post-conciliar Constitutions of the Sisters of St. Joseph affirm the Trinity as the centrality and "fullness of life and union to which all creation is called."[36]

From the earliest days of his conversion, Ignatius experienced many spiritual movements which called for discernment that God's good pleasure might be found. He sought the movements of the Holy Spirit in a maze of winds swaying the spirit to and fro. If the Spirit was at the root of these movements, then the soul felt God's presence in peace and consolation. Through the discernment of spirits, Ignatius became deeply aware of the action of the Holy Spirit within him, and he learned to distinguish this action from other movements arising from "the enemy of mankind." (#334)

With the emphasis on apostolic service and all its demands, the Holy Spirit came to occupy a special place in the spirituality of Ignatius. Discernment of the various spiritual influences took on great importance for a disciple living in and serving the world. Note the similarity of one rule for the Discernment of Spirits for the Second Week in the *Spiritual Exercises* and one of the *Maxims*:

> "It is typical of the evil spirit to transform himself into an angel of light, to go in by the devout soul's way but to come out his own way; I mean he introduces sound and pious thoughts, suited to the piety of that soul; but then, little by little, he tries to achieve his own purposes, by dragging the soul down to his secret designs and corrupt purpose." (#332)

> "Be watchful over yourself and take care not to be deceived by the angel of darkness who masquerades as an angel of light in order to deceive you; and, if your conduct is out of the ordinary, believe that it is not without danger and always mistrust it."

The remainder of Ignatius' life was a continual living out of the trinitarian focus. His was the experience of seeking and finding God in all things, for he saw all things in God. Contemplating God in action became the context and centerpiece of Ignatius' entire life. Fr. Médaille stresses the experience of living in God as opposed to stating a theological position about the Trinity. Hennessey comments:

> "In speaking of the Trinity, Fr. Médaille does not employ the

usual catechetical formula: Father-creation, Son-redemption, Spirit-sanctification.   Instead, he proposes the perfection (will/glory) of the Father, the self-emptying of the Son and the pure and perfect love of the Spirit."[37]

CONSENSUS STATEMENT

Among the French congregations of religious women founded by Jesuits, "only in the instance of the Sisters of St. Joseph is there evidence of a Jesuit actually writing the constitutions of the new congregation."[38]   The heart of this spirituality is contained in the Consensus Statement--the central ideas of Fr. Médaille as found in the Primitive Constitutions:

> "Stimulated by the Holy Spirit of Love and receptive to the Spirit's inspirations, the Sister of St. Joseph moves always towards: profound love of God and love of neighbor without distinction from whom she does not separate herself and for whom, in the following of Christ, she works in order to achieve unity both of neighbor with neighbor and neighbor with God directly in this apostolate and indirectly through works of charity in humility--the spirit of the Incarnate Word in sincere charity (charité cordiale), the manner of St. Joseph whose name she bears in an Ignatian-Salesian climate: that is, with an orientation towards excellence, i.e., le plus which means towards the greater, the magis, tempered by gentleness, peace and joy."[39]

The charism of the Sisters of St. Joseph is embodied in the Consensus Statement. The reference to an "Ignatian-Salesian climate" indicates that the spirituality of St. Francis de Sales was shaped by the *Spiritual Exercises*. The bishop of Geneva (1567-1662) was educated at the Jesuit College of Clermont (and at the University of Padua). Spiritual direction from his school days and throughout his ministry as bishop came from the Society of Jesus. He did the *Spiritual Exercises* each year.[40]   Like St. Ignatius and Fr. Médaille, St. Francis focuses on the universal call to holiness, and his writings are especially practical for the lay person. In his *Introduction to the Devout Life*, he speaks to the contemplative who lives in the world.[41]   Because of the interrelationship of the teaching of St. Ignatius, Fr. Médaille, and

St. Francis de Sales, the founder of the Society of Jesus may be considered the spiritual father of these two men.[42]

Le plus or the magis of the Consensus Statement connotes a meaning broader than mere excellence. The magis is an attitude of mind and heart. Faced with two options both giving equal glory to God, which will I choose? I will choose the alternative which will make me more like Christ. Take for example, the saint who saw two crowns--one of gold, the other of thorns. Assured that her choice would be equally pleasing to Christ, she chose the crown of thorns. Another example is that of a wife who chooses to share a hardship with her husband when he would be equally pleased even if she did not. This explanation deepens the phrase "For the greater glory of God," the English translation of "Ad maiorem Dei gloriam."

THE SPIRITUAL EXERCISES OF ST. IGNATIUS AND THE MAXIMS OF PERFECTION

As a popular literary genre of the seventeenth century, the Maxims summarize the book of the Exercises in "concise statements of practical wisdom."[43] Parallel examples abound between the Maxims and the Exercises. The following is one:

"Spiritual Exercises: For the overcoming of self and the regulation of one's life on the basis of a decision arrived at without any unregulated motive." (#21)

Maxims of Perfection: For those who aspire to the great virtue revised and enlarged by Exercise for stripping self of self, putting on Christ Jesus and imitating him in his hidden and public life in the form of prayers and conversations with the Savior himself by a Servant of God [Fr. Médaille] very enlightened in the interior life. (Frontispiece)

The question naturally arises as to why Fr. Médaille did not directly incorporate the experience of the Exercises into the early spiritual practice of the Sisters of St. Joseph. The early Jesuits were not to undertake the regular spiritual direction of women.[44] Given Fr. Médaille's discretion, he probably chose wisdom when it came to giving the *Exercises* to "*les filles de St Joseph.*"[45] Instead he composed some one hundred maxims for "those aspiring to great virtue." He knew full well that they encapsulated the contents and graces of the *Spiritual Exercises*. We shall see how this is so in Part Three.

Since 1650, the legacy of Fr. Médaille has nurtured the apostolic spirit of thousands of Sisters of St. Joseph who served as "angels of mercy" in the French Revolution, at Gettysburg and in Russia before, during and after the Russian Revolution.[46] Today, in the spirit of Ignatius and Fr. Médaille, there is hardly any ministry in which the Sisters of St. Joseph are not engaged. They have been engaged in education at all levels and in the nursing profession. During the Civil War, Sisters of St. Joseph were 'angels of mercy' on the battlefields of Gettysburg. Since Vatican II, they have expanded their ministries by entering fields of medicine, law, accounting. They are missionaries and social and peace leaders laboring among the poor, the handicapped and downtrodden. Battered women and their children live with Sisters of St. Joseph in residences where they experience the cordial charity so characteristic of the Institute. Sisters of St. Joseph have elevated our culture as musicians and composers, painters, sculptors and poets. Whatever her apostolate, the Sister of St. Joseph shares her inner vision and experience of God with those whom she serves. She loves God *into* her world. Today our Associate Members carry the spirit of Fr. Médaille into a society in need of Christian love.

The *Maxims* and the *Exercises*, like the Scriptures bear within them a timeless message with a contemporary ring. One of our sisters has stated that the maxim, "Desire little in this world and be not overeager for what you may desire," remains a guide for weighing the choices of daily living. Given today's demands on our time and energy, the following two maxims in light of the Ignatian Rules for Discernment offer particularly sound advice:

"Always be serious-minded in your relationship with others; however, let it be a pleasant and gracious seriousness in which there is neither unrestraint nor too much constraint, and seek relaxation, as indeed you should, at the proper time. The bow that is always taut will soon snap."

"Do not become entangled in too many things at once: if, through obedience or some other demand of your work, you have several things to attend to, never be anxious about finishing some in order to work at others. This anxiety troubles peace of heart, causes forgetfulness of God's presence and shows with certainty that there is still much of the old self intermingled with the movements of grace and that nature impedes rather than facilitates what grace would work in us and through us more perfectly if allowed to act with its usual gentleness and with less anxiety on our part about our devotion and health."

Some may view the *Maxims* as outdated piety and irrelevant to a spirituality needed for the future. The *Maxims* should be seen for what they are: a diminutive version of the *Spiritual Exercises*. Although the first Sisters of St. Joseph did not do the full *Exercises*, Fr. Médaille made certain that the *Maxims* contained the world view of the *Spiritual Exercises* in order for them to be lived. Because the *Maxims* from the pre-conciliar *Constitutions* do not follow the order of the *Exercises*, the larger structure of the *Exercises* is not easily recognized by those unfamiliar with the Ignatian handbook. Yet, when the *Maxims* are rearranged, they correspond to every section of the *Exercises*. This will be demonstrated in Part Three.

The *Maxims* depend on the *Spiritual Exercises* for their internal structure; without the latter, the former are Christian aphorisms and instructions disconnected from their original context. In my view, the charism of the Sisters of St. Joseph will not be revitalized without an interior knowledge of the *Spiritual Exercises*. This means doing the *Exercises*. By way of analogy, the following excerpt perhaps explains the present arrangement of the *Maxims*:

"It [is] as though someone took *King Lear* and extracted the great speeches and lyrical passages, arranged them in some rough logical order, dismembered the text, dislocated the dramatic structure and destroyed the story. And then said, there you have the essence of *King Lear*. . . ."[47]

Anne Bernice Hennessey suggests three problems encountered in studying the history and spirituality of the Sisters of St. Joseph: (1) lacunae about the founder, (2) lack of "consistent or scholarly reflection," (3) inability to assemble and edit critical editions of the founder's documents.[48] Yet for years, Sisters of St. Joseph have been aware of the close relationship between their own charism and that of the Society of Jesus and between the *Maxims* and the *Spiritual Exercises*. Sisters have benefited from the experience of either the full *Exercises* (the Thirty-Day Retreat or the Nineteenth Annotation) or the six- or eight-day retreat. Moreover, Sisters of St. Joseph have responded to the ministry of directing men and women retreatants through the *Exercises* while others have entered the field of writing and lecturing on the *Exercises*. The period of refounding necessitates continued study and praying of the *Maxims* and the *Exercises* together.

ARE THE SISTERS OF ST. JOSEPH AN IGNATIAN CONGREGATION?

The preceding reflections have affirmed the thesis of Anne Bernice Hennessey: "The spirituality which Jean-Pierre Médaille proposed for the Sisters of St. Joseph is clearly Ignatian, and therefore apostolic in nature."[49] Let us now summarize by referring more fully to the article entitled "What Is an 'Ignatian Congregation'"?[50] In it, Mary Milligan discusses four ways in which congregations are related to the Society of Jesus:

"1) through reliance on Ignatian texts in the formulation of their own constitution;
2) through influence by individual Jesuits;
3) by modelling certain works or structures on those of the Society of Jesus;
4) by inspiration drawn from Ignatian christological and apostolic visions."[51]

Let us briefly examine these four categories and apply them in varying degrees to the Sisters of St. Joseph.

First, the pre-Vatican II *Constitutions* of the Sisters of St. Joseph relied on Ignatian texts though less so than other congregations. Institutes whose texts bear a close resemblance to the Jesuit Constitutions, have inherited only the Summary of the *Constitutions*, which "resembles a collection of rules".[52] What began as a practical compendium for Jesuit novices was soon promulgated for all Jesuits.[53] Subsequently this *summary* became foundational for many women religious, who followed it as their own constitutions.

Second, the integral relationship between the *Maxims* (and the *Eucharistic Letter*) and the *Spiritual Exercises* intended by Fr. Médaille in the *Primitive Constitutions* is now well established.

Third, the apostolic structures of the Sisters of St. Joseph are based on those of the Society of Jesus. Ignatian retreats continue to be an integral part of the ongoing formation of the Sisters of St. Joseph. As for 'experiments' in the initial formation, sisters in temporary profession are still assigned to so some form of ministry at various intervals to insure the versatility of their training. Moreover, like the Jesuits, the Sisters of St. Joseph from the outset have engaged in an active and mobile apostolate committing themselves to go wherever the need was most pressing--either within the local diocese or in the far off missions.

Lastly, from the teaching of Fr. Médaille, the Sisters of St. Joseph draw their inspiration from a trinitarian and christological theology based on Ignatius' mystical experiences. We may therefore conclude that the Sisters of St. Joseph are an Ignatian congregation.

CONCLUSION

Since Vatican II, religious institutes have deemphasized their individual differences viewing the gospels as their unifying charism. It is true that the gospels represent the pre-eminent charism of all others. Yet the variety of gifts within each religious order refracts the prismatic colors of the gospels as they are incarnated within the entire Catholic Church. Each gospel for example, places a different emphasis on the mystery of Jesus yet each complements the other. No informed Christian would single out one gospel above the others as the embodiment of the full mystery of Jesus. No one of them can encompass a complete understanding of Jesus. Similarly, the unique gifts of the religious orders within the Catholic Church complement each other, for no one religious order can entirely incarnate the mystery and perception of Jesus as the God-Man. Each religious institute enables us to view the mystery of Jesus from a different perspective. In rediscovering their unique charisms, religious orders should seek unity, but unity in diversity.

The Vatican II decree on the renewal of religious life exhorts religious orders and congregations to search out their spiritual roots and rediscover their meaning in light of today's exigencies. The document states:

> "For the good of the Church, institutes must seek after a genuine understanding of their original spirit, so that they will preserve it faithfully when deciding on adaptation, will purify their religious life from alien elements and will free it from what is obsolete."[54]

Like other religious institutes, the Sisters of St. Joseph are preparing to serve the world of the twenty-first century with a renewed spirit. Leaders of the four Federations are promoting a revitalized study of their corporate identity. The key to this realization is to be found in the book and experience of the *Spiritual Exercises* lived by the founder of the Sisters of St. Joseph, Jean-Pierre Médaille of the Society of Jesus.

PART THREE

SPIRITUAL EXERCISES

*To overcome oneself
and to order one's life
without reaching a decision
through some disordered affection.*

MAXIMS OF PERFECTION

*for those
who aspire to the great virtue
revised and enlarged
by*

EXERCISE

*for
stripping self of self,
putting on Christ Jesus
and
imitating him in his hidden and public life
in the form of prayers and conversations
with the Savior himself*

by
a Servant of God
very enlightened in the interior life.
L.R.P.M.D.L.C.D.I.[55]
MDCLXXII

THE SPIRITUAL EXERCISES
and
THE MAXIMS OF PERFECTION

INTRODUCTION

PART THREE BRINGS INTO SHARPER FOCUS THE INTERNAL UNITY between the *Maxims of Perfection* and the *Spiritual Exercises* discussed in Part Two. It bears repeating that neither the *Exercises* nor the *Maxims* were intended as reading material. Like the Scriptures, they were meant to be prayed and lived. Their depth calls for repetition, a practice encouraged by St. Ignatius and Fr. Médaille.

Although their formal structures differ, the *Spiritual Exercises* and the *Maxims of Perfection* present a comprehensive world view of salvation history which is both trinitarian and christological. Both deal with the apostolic nature of prayer. Both make demands on the individual for wholehearted cooperation with the graces contained therein--graces necessary to form the person into a contemplative in action.

CONTEMPLATION IN ACTION. THE CALL TO MYSTICISM

The Christian life is a unity. The Sister of St. Joseph is called to a mysticism lived in the humdrum happenings of every day. Mysticism means nothing less than being in love with God and deepening that love in daily self-offering. A person in love, a worried or angry person carries that love, worry or anger wherever s/he goes. The love, the worry or the anger permeates everything s/he says. People in love cannot help but radiate that love in their entire demeanor. People who have learned the art of unselfish love reflect and point to that divine love to which each of us is called. This is mysticism. This is contemplation in action. Mystics are incarnational people in tune with the earthly as well as the otherworldly; they can find and touch God anywhere--in and through daily occurrences as well as in prayer. They are alive in God.

Jesus is the perfect contemplative in action. His loving union with his Father shone through all he did and said. After spending long hours doing all to please his Father, he withdrew from the crowds to be with his Father in solitude. Action and prayer were two aspects of one reality. One was done for the sake of the other; one flowed from and into the other. The saints loved and labored much doing God's work and with inner peace. First and last they were contemplatives in action.

Apostolic prayer is directly linked to apostolic effectiveness. 'Being with the Lord' includes solitary personal prayer and liturgical prayer, spiritual reading and the daily examen. In these exercises, we develop the style of thinking and acting that is Christ's. Through prayer we assimilate his outlook on life. We put on Christ, a lifelong process and one that comes about from repeatedly 'being with him.' In prayer God's love transforms us into beloved disciples of Jesus. This love-energy becomes the motivation and the lifeblood of our service to others. Prayer fashions us into affective and effective disciples. Fr. Médaille is concise on this point:

> "Recollect yourself frequently in God and do everything in the presence of God."

In our apostolic work, we see, with the eyes of Christ, his Body in the human condition "for Christ plays in ten thousand places. . . ." We become the instruments of God's presence. The apostolate places the disciple in situations which call for multiple decisions made at the faith level, not only in matters of action but those of attitudes, reactions and interractions. Prayer and sensitivity to contemporary culture prepare the disciple for these situations. In the sacrament of the present moment, the demands of the 'market place' test the sincerity of our prayer. We are in the apostolate to please the Lord, to do God's will, and to build up the Body of Christ. The contemplative in action finds God in daily living, pleasant or painful, for the Spirit enlightens, guides and energizes our apostolic endeavors. Listen to Fr. Médaille:

"Continually ponder this truth: that a holy and exemplary life is incomparably more profitable to the neighbor than eloquence. People are more profoundly moved by a saintly example than by words. Besides, God blesses the works of faithful servants more than those of sinners and the imperfect."

"Let your love be active; that is, may it keep loving and urge your heart to keep working for God and for the advancement of God's glory. Then fulfill every demand of this perfect love and at the same time you will have every great virtue and will generously practice them when opportunity arises."

Karl Rahner has said that "the devout Christian disciple of the future will either be a 'mystic,' one who has experienced 'something,' or he will cease to be anything at all."[56]

THE DAILY EXAMEN

In the daily examen, we review the day's experiences, reflecting on whether or not we have found God during the day. The examen provides the opportunity for evaluating time spent with God in prayer and with oneself, and time spent in serving others. The active contemplative combines prayer and activity in alternating movements analogous to the rhythm of nature or that of the sun or tides. Prayer and service are two aspects of the Christian vocation, the one following and flowing into the other. Fr. Médaille speaks to this point:

"Desire the perfection suitable to the three powers of your soul: for the memory, a forgetfulness of all things, even of self, in order to remember God alone; for the seeing of God in all things, the glory, the power, the providence, the mercy of God; for the will, the liberty of approaching God, of loving God and of embracing all the orders of God's providence with all the affection of your soul."

The future will demand much more of us if we are to be apostolically effective. It will require a high degree of personal maturity: availability and mobility, self-containment and the ability to stand on one's own two feet. The Sister of St. Joseph will need to balance solitude, detachment and the finding of God in all things, qualities that are profoundly eremitical, qualities lived not in the cloister but in the world.[57] The following maxims express these thoughts:

> "Take care that God alone be the end and the beginning of all your undertakings and that in carrying them out you never depart from God's divine will; as to their progress, that you be perfectly indifferent whether they succeed or not, desiring in everything and through everything that God's will alone be perfectly accomplished, a will you ought to recognize and love as well in the delaying and failing of your good plans as in their progress and greater success."

> "Notice the different ways great persons and shallow persons act. In order to avoid imperfections of the latter, model yourself on the example of the former. Great persons do everything in great peace; they are like the flowing of the greatest and deepest rivers which, noiselessly are without the slightest hurry, run with unusual swiftness carrying great vessels, enriching and making fertile lands; shallow persons are like small streams that make much noise over the pebbles and yet carry little water and are of little use to the lands they touch; often in time of drought their waters dry up. This is the symbol of shallow persons and the true character of their futile overeagerness in trifling undertakings and works. This is the image of their weak virtue."

Prayer then, is the power of ordinary daily life. Divinity shines through our humanity.

THE SPIRITUAL EXERCISES REVISITED

The experience of Ignatius at the River Cardoner, where he received illuminations into the mystery of the Trinity, forms the graced charism that later impelled him to found the Society of Jesus. The graces Ignatius received from God took shape in a book which he later call the *Spiritual Exercises*. The *Spiritual Exercises* are a charism and a gift not only to the Society of Jesus but to the entire Church as well.

In doing the *Spiritual Exercises*, the exercitant shares in a vicarious way those graces first given to Ignatius. S/he is given graces which parallel those given to Ignatius. A time of deep and prolonged personal prayer, the individual is influenced by and responds to the inner promptings of grace. S/he emerges from the experience more deeply committed to the triune God and to the Lord Jesus made incarnate for us and who "is never separated from the plenitude of being: the Trinity."[58] Covering the expanse of salvation history, the book contains meditations and contemplations, various methods of praying, examinations of conscience, and other spiritual activities.

Like Sts. Benedict, Francis, and Dominic, St. Ignatius founded a school of spirituality. However, unlike their monastic spirituality, his was to be centered in the world. His cosmic view would permeate and transform all sectors of society according to the mind of Christ. Ignatius' personalized vision of God's redemptive plan arose mainly from the infused graces he received at Manresa. Ignatius was a great lover of God. He was also a doer, a born organizer and very practical. He translated his cosmic vision into principles and then into practice. In 1929, Pius XI proclaimed St. Ignatius the patron saint of retreats and "in the encyclical *Mens nostra*, the same pontiff recommended to all the practice of the Ignatian exercises.[59]

LANGUAGE AND STYLE OF THE EXERCISES

The *Exercises* make quite a disappointing first impression, unless one enjoys reading a dry training manual with directions for performing the specified exercises. George Ganss comments:

> [Ignatius] was not a facile writer possessing a style easy to read. When he began to write, his spontaneity seemed to halt. He was a deep and accurate thinker, intent on expressing

exactly what he wanted to say, but simultaneously preoccupied with precautions to be precise and complete. . . . Hence, his style is often difficult, complicated, succinct and sometimes elliptical. . . . His diction is too plain. . . . [Yet] in his own way . . . he was a poetic soul. With emotion he contemplated the flowers, the starry heavens and the deeds of Christ."[60]

It was this same man who, with great ease, could do a Basque dance to cheer up a retreatant in the throes of spiritual distress.

ORGANIZATION OF THE EXERCISES

The *Exercises* are organized in great detail, but here St. Ignatius gives only the general outline of the Weeks of the *Exercises* with their particular themes.

"Four Weeks are taken for the following Exercises, corresponding to the four parts into which they are divided. That is, the First Week is devoted to the consideration and contemplation of sins; the Second, to the life of Christ our Lord up to and including Palm Sunday; the Third, to the Passion of Christ our Lord; and the Fourth, to the Resurrection and Ascension. . . . However, this does not mean that each week must necessarily consist of seven or eight days."[61]

Those who cannot set aside thirty days for the 'Long Retreat,' may do the *Exercises* according to the Nineteenth Annotation. It extends over a period of time, perhaps eight months, and with the guidance of a director, an individual is asked to set aside at least an hour each day to perform a certain exercise.[62] Although details vary with the individual, the end result of the *Exercises* is realized as though one had done the Long Retreat. Today the Nineteenth Annotation has gained wide currency especially because most people cannot leave their responsibilities for a thirty-day retreat. The Nineteenth Annotation enables retreatants to integrate prayer with activity. On the job training! Some have remarked that, instead of having had to curtail their activities during this period, they accomplished far more with time to spare!

The Maxims of Perfection

In the *Maxims*, Fr. Médaille reiterated the centrality of the gospels as the essence of the religious life he lived in the Society of Jesus. He adapted his spirituality for the new Institute in "an innovative yet acceptable manner by women."[63] The whole of Fr. Médaille's spirituality is summarized in the maxim which reads:

> Declare firmly that you will have a tender, strong and
>   constant affection for
> peace and intimate union with God,
> cordial charity and forbearance toward the neighbor,
> humility profound and totally emptied of self,
> the simplicity, gentleness and moderation of the Gospel,
> childlike obedience that does not line up its arguments in
>   advance,
> poverty perfectly stripped,
> mortification discreet and generous, above all,
> very innocent purity of heart which is the foundation for all
>   these beautiful virtues.

Language and Style of the Maxims

Written in the second person, the *Maxims* convey a more spontaneous tone than the dry reserve of the *Exercises*. Sounding more like instructions, they fit well after the various sections of the *Exercises*. If the style of the Exercises is known for its "Spartan terseness,"[64] that of the *Maxims* exudes affectivity. Should distress afflict the individual on or off retreat, the maxims can often dispel the agitation and offer consoling thoughts for the mind, heart and spirit.

Several maxims lend themselves to easy quotation--like proverbs. Some use scriptural and theological language,[65] while others contain practical advice particularly dealing with humility and charity--two virtues closely allied to the vows pronounced by the Sisters of St. Joseph.[66] Some maxims offer unction, others admonition.[67] Regardless of individual character, each maxim carries its own stretch exercise with its own practical twists but never straying from good common sense.[68]

Because of their affectivity, the *Maxims* abound in the use of the comparative and superlative degrees, in asking nothing less than total generosity and commitment of the Sister of St. Joseph. Fr. Médaille speaks consistently of the Ignatian *magis*, and "the most," being "more" pleasing, suffering "everything," "emptying oneself," being "at least in desire, the poorest person, the most gentle and kind . . . ."

CONSECRATION TO THE TWO TRINITIES

The 'maxims' beginning with the word declare, i.e., protest (French translation) have been included in this study because they form the "conclusion of the first part of this little work."[69] The first of these concluding maxims contains the dedication to the twofold Trinity:

> "Consecrate yourself often to the holy and uncreated Trinity of God, Father, Son and Holy Spirit. To the created one of Jesus, Mary and Joseph, and to all the saints of heaven."

Although not contained in the *Maxims* proper, the fuller Consecration to the Two Trinities contained in the *Règlements* is given here:

> [On] the first day of January, they will make a total consecration of themselves to the uncreated and created Trinities, and they will renew together the points that they should profess in honor and in imitation of these dear and glorious Persons, with a generous promise of observing them. They will make this promise and consecration every three months."[70]

The Two Trinities "are exemplars of virtues which may be called relational," . . . not the virtues of the solitary person but the apostolic virtues which reflect the single end of the Ignatian vision of religious life, namely relation to God lived out in directing one's life and those of other people to God--the glory of God and the salvation of souls."[71]

Having provided an overview of the *Exercises* and the *Maxims*, let us turn to the contents proper. First the principal

42

meditations of the Four Weeks of the *Exercises* are presented. The material for prayer includes the grace to be sought, the meditation or contemplation proper, and the colloquy. Those maxims corresponding to the preceding Ignatian exercise follow immediately. Grouped thematically, they restate, summarize, paraphrase or enlarge the main thought of the preceding Ignatian exercise. Some maxims correspond to more than one section of the *Exercises* and therefore have been repeated.[72]

+

FIRST WEEK

Spiritual Exercises: Principle and Foundation

Human beings have been created to praise, reverence and serve our Lord God, and by means of this to save their souls.

The other things on the face of the earth are created for the human beings to help them in attaining the end for which we are created.

From this it follows that I should use these things to the extent that they help me toward my end, and rid myself of the them to the extent that they hinder me.

To do this, I must make myself indifferent to all created things, in regard to everything which is left to my freedom of will and is not forbidden. Consequently, on my own part I ought not to seek health rather than sickness, wealth rather than poverty, honor rather than dishonor, a long life rather than a short life, and so on in all other matters.

I ought to desire and elect only the thing which is more conducive to the end for which I am created.[73](SE: #23)

Daily Particular Examination of Conscience (SE: #24-26) The Daily Examen may be found in Part Four beginning on page seventy-seven.

+

Maxims of Perfection: Principle and Foundation

The following maxims include themes such as the Christian vocation, detachment, indifference, and freedom for all earthly affection, contentment, purity of intention, longings and desires, peace and Divine Providence.

1. Have always in sight the great end of your Christian commitment; see your particular vocation and the movement of divine grace which draws you gently and firmly to live the great virtue; and do nothing which might distance you from or make you undeserving of the graces with which God in the divine goodness has been favoring you perhaps for some time and with little fruitfulness.

2. Have God alone before your eyes, God's unique contentment and glory, and attach no importance whatsoever to anything else.

3. Always be perfectly predisposed to receive with gentleness and indifference everything that is not contrary to God: to be healthy or sick, happy or dissatisfied, loved or persecuted; to do one thing or the other; to live or to die; in a word, predisposed to receive the whole of God's will for you which you ought to love tenderly whatever it may be. All that comes from the hand of God is very beneficial when we receive it properly.

4. Be filled with sentiments of indifference, of resignation to the will of God, of abandonment into God's hands, of total acquiescence to all the orders of Divine Providence, of tender love for these orders, and of the complete accomplishment of all God desires of you, constantly doing and bearing what God wishes and, as best you can, in the way God wishes: these are the acts which encompass and explain the total conformity of our will to the divine will and constitute the perfection of love and of our entire holiness.

5. Declare firmly in honor of God the Holy Spirit that you will free your heart from the love of every created being in order to fill it with the pure and perfect love of God and to do

everything in the constant practice of this holy love.

6. Free yourself from every affection on earth and so empty your heart that no created being holds it back. A heart empty of all is, at the same time, full of God.

7. Take care that God alone be the end and the beginning of all your undertakings and that in carrying them out you never depart from God's divine will; as to their progress, that you be perfectly indifferent whether they succeed or not, desiring in everything and through everything that God's will alone be perfectly accomplished, a will you ought to recognize and love as well in the delaying and failing of your good plans as in their progress and greater success.

8. Love nothing but God and what can be called God's. Be wholly given to God by a complete self-abandonment to divine Providence; wholly for God by a love pure and completely selfless; wholly in God by the constant deepening awareness of his presence; wholly according to God by a perfect conformity of your every desire and of the state of your life to the beloved ordering of the divine will alone.

9. Make once and for all such a perfect sacrifice of your will to God that you no longer allow yourself deliberately to wish for anything except that God's holy will always be done in you and through you.

10. Seek in everything you do that God be content and nothing else, and in practicing this maxim throughout your life, in sickness, desolation, persecution and similar events, desire solely what contents God more without concern for your own interests.

11. Be just as content that others are more intelligent and gifted than you, even more virtuous and grace-filled when this is God's will; you ought on the one hand to judge yourself least worthy of these same graces, and on the other to adore all of God's ways and to rest your contentment in the accomplishment of God's good pleasure alone.

12. Concerning purity of intention, may you be nothing to yourself, utterly given to God and to the neighbor, for God and according to God, and that you act constantly with these feelings which bring you to a perfect purity in living out your intentions.

13. In living your life have only one desire: to be and to become the person God wills you to be in nature, in grace, and in glory for time and for eternity.

14. Desire little in this world and be not overeager for what you may desire.

15. In order to acquire this peace and this serenity of spirit, live in a perfect purity of heart; do not cling to anything created; continually struggle to calm the restless impulses of your passions; avoid also excessive fear and scruples. Live without desire and without fixed plan, completely given over to God and to the guidance of persons superior to you.

16. Regard as particularly suspect any desire which is too overeager and capable of disturbing your peace or diverting you from more necessary and more obligatory works.

17. Be nothing to yourself, utterly given to God and to the neighbor, for God and according to God, and that you act constantly with these feelings which bring you to a perfect purity in living out your intentions.

18. Be sad if you notice that people turn their attention to you, esteem you, have affection for you, and believe in truth that these thoughts and affections are put to poor use: be sad, furthermore, that Christians misuse their love when they cling to created things; and desire, as indeed you should, that every thought and affection of men and angels, for time and eternity, be solely of God or solely for God.

19. Never ask for anything, never refuse anything unless you judge it absolutely necessary after having entrusted the matter to God; even in that case, do so by a simple proposal

46

and with indifference and total resignation as to whether your request is accepted or refused.

20. Never think of the future unless it is somehow necessarily related to your present work: entrust everything to the Providence of God your Father.

21. Act in such a way that your good works are hidden in time to be revealed only in eternity or to be known only by God alone and never by others if God so wills. If you act in the sentiments of this maxim, your love will be more pleasing in God's eyes and your intention more perfect and detached; and this is what you ought to seek.

+

Spiritual Exercises: Sin

I ask God our Lord for the grace that all my intentions, actions and operations may be ordered purely to the service and praise of his Divine Majesty. (SE: #46)

Colloquy. Imagine Christ our Lord suspended before you, and converse with him in colloquy: How is it that he, although he is the Creator, has come to make himself a human being? How is it that he has passed from eternal life to death here in time, to die in this way for my sins?
In a similar way, reflect on yourself and ask: What have I done for Christ? What am I doing for Christ? What ought I to do for Christ?
In this way, too, gazing on him in so pitiful a state as he hangs on the cross, speak out whatever comes to your mind. (SE: #53)

+

Maxims of Perfection: Sin

1. After success in good works, admit that your inadequate fidelity to grace and the sins committed result in much less progress than God expected from your cooperation.

2. Begin by a total purifying of your heart and your conscience; atone for your past sins through penance and tears; uproot any bad habits; overcome them generously by practicing the opposite; free yourself of the least fault and willful imperfection; and even avoid any occasion in which you will have reason to fear some chance of falling into sin. Until a heart is wholly purified, it will not readily receive the great communications of grace necessary for the practice of the great virtue.

3. Believe that in the whole living out of your life, you do nothing but prevent the beloved workings of grace and diminish its fruitfulness and consequences.

4. Do not have the slightest esteem for yourself or for your actions; be convinced rather that if you really knew yourself and the imperfection present in all you do, you would have a perfect lack of esteem for yourself and real difficulty in bearing with yourself.

5. However pure your intentions seem, believe that in some hidden recess of your heart you always seek your self and that your nature is always intermingled with the workings of grace. Oh, how rarely is virtue entirely free of self-love.

6. In order to become more humble, judge in truth that you are only nothing, illusion and sin: nothing in your own being; sin in the many offenses that you have so often committed and that you commit daily; illusion in the esteem that others have for you and for your actions which are certainly illusions since they have more the appearance than the reality of good and are often praised by others when they deserve much blame.

7. Never complain except about yourself; always accuse yourself and excuse others.

8. Work then at tempering all your passions; keep struggling with them until you have completely subjected them to the guidance of reason and the enlightenments of grace.

9. Consider the loss which disobedience to grace has caused you: if this were completely known to you, you would die of grief; you could not go on living; avoid any such loss in the future and make better use of the graces of the Holy Spirit.

✢

SECOND WEEK

Spiritual Exercises: The Call of the Temporal King as an Aid toward Contemplating the Life of the Eternal King

I will ask the grace from our Lord that I may not be deaf to his call, but ready and diligent to accomplish his most holy will. (SE: #91)

Those who desire to show greater devotion and to distinguish themselves in total service to their eternal King and universal Lord will not only offer their persons for the labor, but go further still. They will work against their human sensitivities and against their carnal and worldly love, and they will make offerings of greater worth and moment and say: (SE: #97)

"Eternal Lord of all things, I make my offering, with your favor and help, I make it in the presence of your infinite Goodness, and of your glorious Mother, and of all the holy men and women in your heavenly court. I wish and desire, and it is my deliberate decision, provided only that it is for your greater service and praise, to imitate you in bearing all injuries and affronts, and any poverty, actual as well as spiritual, if your Most Holy Majesty desires to elect and receive me into such a life and state." (SE: #98)

✢

Maxims of Perfection: The Call of the Temporal King as an Aid toward Contemplating the Life of the Eternal King; the More.
The following maxims have as their theme God's greater glory.[74]

1. Declare firmly in honor of God the Father that you will practice what, according to your knowledge, is the more perfect; what you believe corresponds to God's greater glory and to the greater contentment of the sovereign Majesty.[75]

2. In everything about your state of life and in all your actions, desire if it glorifies God more and you are not undeserving of it, to please God as much as the greatest saints who lived or are living and who practiced or are practicing these same actions: but may this desire have its source in an unselfish love which seeks nothing but God's contentment.

3. Follow through on good works that you undertake until they are almost completed and then, if it can be done conveniently, have someone else complete them and get the glory before others, and you will have greater glory before God.

4. Desire no praise or reward whatsoever for your good works in this life and you will have more perfect and greater in eternity. Oh, how meaningless esteem and reward for our actions in this world lessen their merit in the other.

5. See your greatness in God and your nothingness in your self so that the sight of your weakness and of that nothingness may ceaselessly humble you and confound you, and so that your greatness in God may bring you to desire nothing but what is great, to live every excellent virtue in its more perfect expression, to make the least action great by a great love of God and by a perfect purity and nobility of intention.

6. In order to further your desire to become holy and to support you in living continually the more perfect virtues, often contemplate God in the divine and infinite perfections; you will find in them such awesome perfection, such merits, and so many demands to serve God perfectly that the least slackening or mediocrity in God's holy service will deeply pain you and the difficulties or contradictions met in the exercising of great holiness will never weary you.

7. Just as you ought to be courageous in undertaking all that God desires of you for God's glory and for the good of others, so also you ought to remain constant in your undertakings, never giving them up whatever opposition you may encounter unless you are completely unable to do anything more about them, and according to this maxim.

8. Calmly yet energetically continue to the end what you have determined and prudently judged to be in accordance with the greater glory of God.

9. Take as your life principle to be perfect as your heavenly Father is perfect; therefore, in each instance, courageously choose to live what you will believe to be the more perfect, what will correspond to the greater glory of God your Father, what will be more pleasing in his sight and more according to God's holy will.

10. When there is a question of doing many things at the same time either in your private homes or in some community gathering, if you are given a choice, choose what will be more degrading, even more difficult, leaving to others what is more honorable and easier.

11. The true motto of a person whom God mercifully chooses to use for his glory or on whom God showers loving blessings should be this of St. Paul: "I am what I am by the grace of my God," or that of St. Teresa after the Royal Prophet: I will forever sing the mercies of God."

12. In your works be on guard against seeking the satisfaction or consolation that accompany the trials of those who work for the advancement of God's glory and for the salvation of others: desire only that God be glorified, that the neighbor be enlightened, saved and perfected, and never in any way look for the satisfaction and sweetness found when one sees one's works succeed. That is the end which you ought to envision in living out your life and the principle which will help you to be perfect as your heavenly Father is perfect.

Spiritual Exercises: The Incarnation

I ask for an interior knowledge of our Lord, who became human for me, that I may love him more and follow him more intensely and follow him more closely. (SE: #104)

Colloquy. At the end a colloquy should be made. I will think over what I ought to say to the Three Divine Persons, or to the eternal Word made flesh, or to our Mother and Lady. I will beg favors according to what I feel in my heart, that I may better follow and imitate Our Lord, who in this way has recently become a human being. (SE: # 109)

+

Maxims of Perfection: Incarnation and the Life of Our Lord

The maxims on the Incarnation include the imitation of Christ, transformation into Christ by the emptying of oneself, and the vow and virtue of obedience.

1. Empty yourself constantly in honor of the Incarnate Word who lovingly emptied himself for you. In this self-emptying, profess the most sincere and profound humility that you come to know.

2. In the same spirit of the Savior Jesus, live a life hidden in God in order to practice great interior acts such as adoration, admiration, glorification, reverence, love and in order to draw from that life the spirit of the great virtue of humility, to which we can readily be led only by grace and by the imitation of Jesus who is our way, our truth and our life.

3. By this transformed life in Christ Jesus, love what the world hates; hate what the world loves; let the world be crucified to you and you to it: empty yourself completely of the spirit of the world and be filled with Christ Jesus and with the fullness of his holy Spirit; and more specifically, in order to live more fully the life of the Savior Jesus.

4. Put aside your old self so that you can put on the new and, in order to live in the perfection of this maxim, die to every form of pride and every movement of the heart which originates in a wounded nature rebellious to the grace of the Holy Spirit. Being thus dead to nature and to the old self, live the life of Christ Jesus putting on his humility, his gentleness, his simplicity and his other virtues so that with St. Paul you may exclaim, "I live; no, it is no longer I who live; it is Christ Jesus who lives in me."

5. Put on and be completely filled with Jesus, interiorly applying his graces, merits, intentions and all the holiness of his virtues, and exteriorly manifesting his gentleness, modesty, simplicity and his adorable humility.

6. Do everything in Jesus, uniting yourself to him as a branch to its vine: in fact, he says that he is the vine, we the branches. Do everything with Jesus, united to him as the instrument of its principal cause or as the hand of the apprentice to that of the master who guides it. Do everything through Jesus, desiring that all you do have its source only in him and that he be the soul of your soul, the life of your life and the spirit which animates your every action.

7. Declare firmly in honor of God the Son that you will try to imitate his total self-emptying and totally empty yourself of self.

8. Declare firmly in honor of the Savior Jesus that you will put aside your old self so that you can put on the new, namely Christ Jesus himself, living insofar as you can, by his life and in the perfect imitation of his virtues.

9. Declare firmly in honor of the Blessed Virgin who was full of grace and used that grace so well that, in imitation of her, you will be perfectly faithful to every grace of the Holy Spirit.

On Obedience

10. Obey those superior to you as you would God and not as you would others. This advice of St. Paul profoundly embraced will raise you in a short time to the perfection of obedience.

11. Perform your actions with faithful care; avoid the least imperfection in them, and do what is necessary to guarantee all the conditions needed to perform them: one action well done is worth a thousand done halfheartedly. On this point, remember in living your life to give yourself seriously and wholeheartedly to do the present will of God without distracting yourself about the future, a common illusion used by Satan to divert you from the attention required for your present actions; thus they are full of imperfection.

12. When something is commanded, obey faithfully, joyfully and simply and, if possible, without permitting the slightest thought of repugnance or refusal or without interjecting a single word between the order and the execution of the command.

13. Recognize and tenderly love this very pure will of God in all the events of your life, however trying they may be, and in all the commands of persons superior to you unless there is danger of sin in these commands.

14. Be especially careful in executing what the people who are superior to you recommend or what pertains to your duty, particularly when it affects the good of the group to which you belong or what is helpful and necessary to the neighbor. And notice the fact that often we habitually defer doing this in order to do that which is less in the line of duty and more in keeping with our whims and petty interests.

15. Do not ask about the arrangements superior persons have to make of you: await them with serenity and patience as from the hands of God and desire that they be made known to you only when God so chooses without being overeager to

discover them beforehand.

16. If you are in religion, live content with the work assigned by your superiors: carefully apply your mind and heart to it without the slightest thought of change until the moment obedience ordains it.

17. Believe the truth that Divine Providence leads persons less advanced through those superior to them and thus moves them to follow without deviation from the sure road destined for them: convinced of this, you will obey without difficulty, and you will not dare contradict the will of those who hold the place of God on earth and who only command in God's name lest you stray from the path of your salvation.

18. In particular, declare firmly that, like them, you will have a tender, strong and constant affection for
peace and intimate union with God,
cordial charity and forbearance toward the neighbor,
humility profound and totally emptied of self,
the simplicity, gentleness and moderation of the Gospel,
childlike obedience that does not line up its arguments in
advance,
poverty perfectly stripped,
mortification discreet and generous,
above all, very innocent purity of heart which is the
foundation for all these beautiful virtues.

+

Spiritual Exercises: A Meditation on the Two Standards and the Discernment of Spirits

I ask for insight into the deceits of the evil leader, and for help to guard myself against them; and further, for insight into the genuine life which the supreme and truthful commander sets forth, and grace to imitate him. (SE: #139)

It is characteristic of the evil angel who takes on the appearance of an angel of light, to enter by going along with the devout soul and then to come out by his own way with success for himself. That is, he brings good and holy thoughts attractive to such an upright person and then strives little by little to get his own way, by enticing the soul over to his own hidden deceits and evil intentions. (SE: #332)

The First Colloquy should be with Our Lady. I beg her to obtain for me grace to be received under the standard of her Son and Lord; that is, to be received, first, in the highest degree of spiritual poverty and also, if his Divine Majesty would be served and if he should wish to choose me for it, to no less degree of actual poverty; and second, in bearing reproaches and injuries, that through them I may imitate him more, if only I can do this without sin on anyone's part and without displeasure to his Divine Majesty. Then I will say a Hail Mary.

The Second Colloquy. It will be to ask the same grace from the Son, that he may obtain it for me from the Father. Then I will say the Soul of Christ [*Anima Christi*] on page eighty-five.

The Third Colloquy will be to ask the same grace from the Father, that he may grant it to me. Then I will say an Our Father. (SE: #147)

+

Maxims of Perfection: A Meditation on the Two Standards and the Discernment of Spirits

The following maxims speak of discerning the choices one makes at the level of faith. They recommend a wise and prudent director. They give advice for personal discernment and fidelity to grace. They apply the rules for discernment to practical matters for self and one's apostolic ministry.

1. Be watchful over yourself and take care not to be deceived by the angel of darkness who masquerades as an angel of light in order to deceive you; and, if your conduct is out of

the ordinary, believe that it is not without danger and always mistrust it.

2.   In order to walk more securely on the spiritual way, choose a wise director; be candid in revealing to him or her the deepest part of you; follow his [her] guidance and advice and do nothing of importance without his [her] direction.

3.   Be constant once you have chosen the direction of your life changing nothing unless a wise director deems it necessary for a greater perfection in your manner of living or for the correction of what is imperfect in it.

4.   Live and act according to reason and duty and not according to whim or the rash movement of some inclination.

5.   Live in peace and interior gentleness always and show it outwardly by acting without haste or overeagerness.   Even suffer what you have to suffer peacefully in perfect repose of spirit in God and in loving acceptance of all the plans of his divine will.

6.   Desire for your body a perfect submission of its imagination and all of its senses to the direction of reason.

7.   Always be serious-minded in your relationship with others; however, let it be a pleasant and gracious seriousness in which there is neither unrestraint nor too much constraint, and seek relaxation, as indeed you should, at the proper time, at the proper time.   The bow that is always taut will soon snap.

8.   Do not become entangled in too many things at once: if, through obedience or some other demand of your work, you have several things to attend to, never be anxious about finishing some in order to work at others.   This anxiety troubles peace of heart, causes forgetfulness of God's presence and shows with certainty that there is still much of the old self intermingled with the movements of grace and that nature impedes rather than facilitates what grace would work in us and through us more perfectly if allowed to act with its usual

gentleness and with less anxiety on our part about our devotion and health.

9. Desire the perfection for your higher faculties: for the memory, a general forgetting of all that is not God or does not tend towards God; for the understanding, a simple vision of God and of his adorable good pleasure in all things so that it sees all solely in God and nothing outside of God; for the will, the sole freedom to go to God, to love God, to depend on God and to embrace all the orders of the divine will.

10. Obey faithfully the movements of grace; there are few people who give faithful obedience to grace. Often they respond sluggishly and negligently, seldom fully accomplishing the good that God inspires in them.

11. Those who readily let God act in them and through them without too much self-interference do a great many things in a short time and never loses peace of heart.

12. When you experience the sweetness of sensible grace and have the good fortune to experience tender consolation, keep in mind that this grace is loaned to you rather than given; that it belongs less to you than to the Savior Jesus who earned it through his merits; that the same Savior can take it from you whenever he pleases without any injustice to you, especially if you become unworthy of it; and that if, in his divine plan, he is not, however, obliged to share himself so lavishly with you; and that, when he does, it comes from the overflow of his divine mercy which should confound you, knowing how undeserving you are and that you constantly misuse his boundless gifts.

13. Hold it as certain and as an infallible maxim that you are not holier when you commit fewer faults and practice virtue more readily but that you are more indebted to God and God's grace which often makes beginners more fervent in good works and less apt to fail than those already well advanced. Neither should you believe that holiness consists in being endowed with many gifts, favored with sensible graces and led

by extraordinary means on the path of virtue; all this may be found as well in a person who has many imperfections and hidden weaknesses and who, in countless situations foreseen by God, might allow herself to be overcome by temptation. Real holiness consists in something well hidden, known to God alone and you are still far from it as much as you believe ever so slightly that you have reached it.

14. Hope for all good things which you expect from the divine mercy with a confidence as certain as if you already possessed them: but rest your hope on God's goodness, his fidelity to his promises, the merits of the Savior Jesus and on your fidelity to the graces of this divine Savior. For God, who made you without you, will not save you without you; that is to say, God will not save you if you do not profit these graces by the good use of your free will.

15. In order to direct your self more exactly toward fidelity, consider carefully that resistance to grace, however slight, interferes amazingly with the flow of grace upon our own progress in the virtue and upon the good works directed toward the glory of God and the benefit of the neighbor. And what makes us stop and think is the fact that one particular infidelity to grace marked the beginning of eternal punishment for many: let us dread that a similar misfortune befall us.

16. In the difficulties and contradictions met in carrying out your laudable undertakings, strengthen yourself against the dread of human fear and do not permit your heart to be overcome. When it seems that everything from the divine goodness and, in order to enliven your confidence, believe, as indeed you should, that, if your plans are of God, they will succeed sooner or later, and opposition will serve only to confirm or perfect them. If they are not of God, you ought to be the first to desire that they be opposed and that others work to destroy them; besides, they cannot possibly last if they are not of God since the Savior Jesus has said that every seedling not planted by his heavenly Father will be pulled up by the roots.

17. Never consider events, however trying, as obstacles but as very beneficial and necessary to living your life: if you view them as the effects of a very gentle, loving Providence of God your Father on your behalf, you will love them tenderly and receive them willingly.

18. Notice the different ways great persons and shallow persons act. In order to avoid imperfections of the latter, model yourself on the example of the former. Great persons do everything in great peace; they are like the flowing of the greatest and deepest rivers which, noiselessly are without the slightest hurry, run with unusual swiftness carrying great vessels, enriching and making fertile lands; shallow persons are like small streams that make much noise over the pebbles and yet carry little water and are of little use to the lands they touch; often in time of drought the true character of their futile overeagerness in trifling undertakings and works. This is the image of their weak virtue."

19. Whatever virtue you recognize in yourself, never lose a genuine fear of God, convinced that the judgments of God are fathomless and that they are quite different from human judgments; that St. Paul feared that he would not be justified even though he could see nothing within himself to warrant that fear; that he was apprehensive lest, while preaching to others, he might be lost; and that Scripture advises us to humble ourselves under the all-powerful hand of God and to work out our salvation in fear and trembling.

20. Interpret all things kindly and in the most favorable sense.

21. Work then at tempering all your passions; keep struggling with them until you have completely subjected them to the guidance of reason and the enlightenments of grace.

60

Spiritual Exercises: Three Ways of Being Humble

The First Way of Being Humble is necessary for eternal salvation, and consists in this. I so lower and humble myself, as far as is in my power, that in all things I may be obedient to the law of God our Lord.

Consequently, even though others would make me lord of all creatures in the world, or even though to save my temporal life, I would not enter into deliberation about violating a commandment either human or divine which binds me under mortal sin.

The Second Way of Being Humble is more perfect than the first. It is what I have when I find myself in this disposition. When the options seem equally effective for the service of God our Lord and the salvation of my soul, I do not desire or feel myself strongly attached to have wealth rather than poverty, or honor rather than dishonor, or a long life rather than a short one.

Furthermore, neither for all creation nor to save my life would I enter into deliberation about committing a venial sin.

The Third Way of Humility is the more perfect and consists in this. When I possess the first and second ways, and when the options equally further the praise and glory of God, in order to imitate Christ our Lord better and to be more like him here and now, I desire and choose poverty with Christ poor rather than wealth; contempt with Christ laden with it rather than honors. Even further, I desire to be regarded as a useless fool for Christ, who before me was regarded as such, rather than as a wise or prudent person in this world. (SE: #165-167)

+

Maxims of Perfection: Humility

These maxims place before us Jesus as the model of humility. Mary and Joseph are also models for us. Humility is necessary in our dealings with others.

1.   Empty yourself constantly in honor of the Incarnate Word who lovingly emptied himself for you.   In this self-emptying, profess the most sincere and profound humility that you come to know.

2.   Declare firmly in honor of God the Son that you will try to imitate his total self-emptying and totally empty yourself of self.

3.   Declare firmly in honor of the glorious St. Joseph that you will serve and love Jesus and Mary wholeheartedly as he served and loved them, and that when you serve the neighbor, you will do so in Joseph's spirit of humility, gentleness and charity.

4.   So act, as St. Paul says, that with Christ Jesus your whole life be hidden in God.   That is to say, do everything in God and with God by the practice of an interior life animated with the sovereign intentions of God when your actions are prescribed and you are helped to execute them well.   In everything, desire to be filled, led and, as it were, animated by the Holy Spirit who is truly the soul of our soul since it lives by God through grace and is, as it were, deified by God.   Oh, if only you knew how to live in the fullness of the Spirit of Jesus in God, and in fullness of the Spirit of God with the Savior Jesus, what progress would you not make in every kind of grace, virtue and merit for eternity!

5. Put aside your old self so that you can put on the new and, in order to live in the perfection of this maxim, die to every form of pride and every movement of the heart which originates in a wounded nature rebellious to the grace of the Holy Spirit.   Being thus dead to nature and to the old self, live the life of Christ Jesus putting on his humility, his gentleness, his simplicity and his other virtues so that with St. Paul you may exclaim, "I live; no, it is no longer I who live; it is Christ Jesus who lives in me."

6.   Put on and be completely filled with Jesus, interiorly applying his graces, merits, intentions and all the holiness of his

virtues, and exteriorly manifesting his gentleness, modesty, simplicity and his adorable humility.

7.　Base the whole strength and hope of success in whatever you plan upon a complete mistrust of self that you ought to join to a perfect confidence in God alone.　Practice such acts of mistrust especially at the beginning of your every action.　And, in order to combine prudence with sentiments of a true humility:　although you should expect everything from God in whatever you undertake, nevertheless be as diligent in carrying out your good works as if all depended on your effort alone and as if God had entrusted their success to your watchfulness alone and to your work.

8.　Humble yourself, empty yourself constantly before God and before others; believe yourself undeserving of all things good and deserving of all evil; reverence God's judgments which are so very different from human judgments; have an extreme horror of praise and esteem from others; love contempt, seek it, and accept the truth that great persons find a priceless treasure of grace and heavenly consolation in being humbled when they accept it properly; and so, bless God with a spirit full of joy whenever you are forsaken, disdained, contradicted or little esteemed by others.　These are the sentiments of humility the saints lived, the humility you ought to make your own in the well-founded conviction that their virtue was incomparably greater than your own and that, contrasted with their outstanding holiness, your whole life is full of imperfection.

9.　Be at least in desire, the poorest person in the world, the most gentle and kind, the humblest, the most persevering; in a word, the most perfect in the practice of every virtue of which he has left us the example in his holy life and, in a special way, in his death.

10.　Hide in the best way you can the few graces God sees fit to give you, revealing them with much modesty, simplicity and humility only to your spiritual director.　On the other hand, if the opportunity arises, reveal what is apt to cause you to be less esteemed as long as this is done discretely and without violating the laws of prudence, obedience and charity.

11. Never speak of yourself, whether for good or for ill, without real necessity, in which case you will try to bring much simplicity and prudence to what you have to say so that you contribute nothing untimely or vain.

12. In order not to lose the fruit of your good works and in order to merit the grace of persevering in them: shun with an extreme horror any self-complacency that you might find in them and give all the glory to God and to our Savior Christ Jesus who, by his death, has become the source and very heart of your supernatural life and of all your praiseworthy actions.

13. Desire that others be held in high regard and be content that, in everything, others are preferred to you.

14. Be just as content that others are more intelligent and gifted than you, even more virtuous and grace-filled when this is God's will; you ought on the one hand to judge yourself least worthy of these same graces, and on the other to adore all of God's ways and to rest your contentment in the accomplishment of God's good pleasure alone.

15. Rejoice in all things over the unique glory of God regardless whom you see promoting it: it is a great illusion on the part of some zealous persons to want to do everything themselves or have it done by their associates, and to be unable to tolerate that others succeed in their undertakings and in the care they take to make God known and glorified. Whoever remains of this mind is very far from the pure love of God and true humility which causes one to be just as content and even more content when it appears that others advance in glory than if one seems to be advancing it similarly oneself and which prefers incomparably to see engaged in works of zeal those who bring God a glory greater than or equal to what one might bring God if one were engaged in those holy works oneself.

64

16. See your greatness in God and your nothingness in your self so that the sight of your weakness and of that nothingness may ceaselessly humble you and confound you, and so that your greatness in God may bring you to desire nothing but what is great, to live every excellent virtue in its more perfect expression, to make the least action great by a great love of God and by a perfect purity and nobility of intention.

17. Declare firmly that you will have a tender, strong and constant affection for
> peace and intimate union with God,
> cordial charity and forbearance toward the neighbor,
> humility profound and totally emptied of self,
> the simplicity, gentleness and moderation of the Gospel,
> childlike obedience that does not line up its arguments in advance,
> poverty perfectly stripped,
> mortification discreet and generous,
> above all, very innocent purity of heart which is the foundation for all these beautiful virtues.

+

THIRD WEEK

Spiritual Exercises   The Passion and Death of Jesus

I ask for heartfelt sorrow and confusion, because the Lord is going to his Passion for my sins. (SE: #193)

I ask for what I desire. Here it is what is proper for the Passion: sorrow with Christ in sorrow; a broken spirit with Christ so broken; tears; and interior suffering because of the great suffering which Christ endured for me. (SE: #203)

Colloquy. Finish with a colloquy to Christ our Lord, and at its end recite an Our Father.

+

Maxims of Perfection: The Passion and Death of Jesus

The following maxims express the graces sought for in the Third Week. They describe what the attitude of the disciple ought to be toward suffering.

1. Believe the truths of the Gospel with an even stronger faith when they are more difficult to understand: but believe them with a living faith which grasps, as is necessary, the unutterable and awesome mysteries of our holy religion.

2. Christ Jesus ennobled and divinized suffering in his person and, since his death, suffering ennobled and divinized through him, ennobles and divinizes those who use it well.

3. Choose to endure every trial of time rather than the least trial of eternity: every trial of nature rather than the least privation of grace: and, in keeping with this maxim based entirely on the supernatural light of faith, embrace the loss of every good and the endurance of every trial rather than fail in any respect to fulfill the very holy will of God.

4. Endure without murmuring, without complaining so as to make your suffering too noticeable; without seeking relief except when necessary so as not to displease God; without letting yourself be too carried away by interior sadness or exterior anxiety; without tiring of suffering; desiring to endure more if such were God's good pleasure; with thanksgiving, joy, pleasure and in this truth: that everything you can possibly endure is nothing compared to the punishment you have merited by your sins and compared to what Jesus endured for you. If you profit by this advice, you will be happy in your suffering and your reward will be very great in heaven, especially if you continually unite all your pain and your trials to those of Jesus crucified.

5. If you should be abandoned by creatures and even by God through the withdrawal of sensible graces, remember the abandonment of Jesus himself on the cross and tenderly love yours remembering his.

6. Live with the saints at the Cross, die to pleasure and at the same time you will live to God and die entirely to yourself.

7. Love suffering in its pure form: that is to say, suffering where there is nothing but suffering, stripped of every kind of exterior and interior consolation. This is most like the suffering of the Savior Christ Jesus especially the suffering of his Passion.

8. Suffering well received is like wood which feeds the fire of divine love: as you faithfully endure more, using your suffering well, you will experience the sacred fire of this love spreading in your heart, and persons who posses this great love are usually led along the path of great suffering: grasp this truth and profit by it. A great fire can hardly keep burning unless one keeps throwing much wood on it; in the same way, in order to sustain a great love of God throughout life, one must endure great pain.

9. The real proof of love is to endure much for those one loves. Endure much for God and you will show that you love God much. If you do not want to suffer anything for God, it is a sign that you do not love God.

10. When crushed by great affliction, do not yearn for death (although you may wish for it solely according to the plan of God's good pleasure); let it suffice for you to be crucified with Jesus as much as, and in the way, it pleases him, and to die on your cross at the moment Divine Providence will have completed in you, through you and by you what he will have destined to accomplish both in the living of your life and in the hour and the manner of your death. It will be at that moment, through a happy *consummatum est* pronounced in imitation and if possible in the spirit of the Savior Jesus, that you will deliver your soul happily into the hands of your heavenly Father to enter into the presence of his glory and to enjoy in heaven an eternal reward in keeping with the nature, merit and number of your works.

11.   If your state of life does not allow you to work openly for the advancement of God's glory and the salvation of the neighbor, offer for both of these aims your holy desires, your prayers, your tears and your penances; in a word, every work of your life and the agony of your death, uniting them with the holy intentions of the Savior Jesus who lived and died for his dear Father and for us who effected, especially on the Cross, the adorable mystery of our redemption.

12.   In order to suffer fruitfully, desire to do so with the holy attitude and patience of the Savior Jesus and, to be specific, suffer in this manner which is the perfection of the Christian patience.

13.   In the practice of hope, trust God all the more when, in trials and sorrows, human help seems less apparent. However, in your greatest afflictions, dangers and difficulties do not always hope that God will deliver you, comfort you or bring about the success of your undertakings; but hope that God will do in you and with you the divine will. Live content with this thought.

14.   Join to the endurance of suffering that come to you the voluntary seeking of many others through the practice of mortification which must be prudent as to the physical but which can never be too great as to the passions, inordinate affections and other tendencies of a nature which should be constantly mortified in order to be able to live the life of the spirit.

15.   In this greatheartedness, consider whatever you may be able to do and suffer for God as insignificant: for in fact everything is nothing before God, and however great may be our service of God it is always very lowly and insignificant in the light of what God infinitely deserves.

+

FOURTH WEEK

Spiritual Exercises: The Resurrection

I pray for the grace to be glad and rejoice intensely because of the great joy and the glory of Christ our Lord. (SE: #221)

Colloquy.   Finish with a colloquy, according to the subject matter, and recite the Our Father.

✝

Maxims of Perfection: The Resurrection

The maxims of the Resurrection express joy, love and wholeheartedness.

1.   As you should love God above everything and everything for God: so should you love in God, with a strong and tender love, the divinized humanity of the Savior Jesus to whom you are infinitely indebted, the Blessed Virgin our good Mother, her dear husband St. Joseph, and her holy parents, together with all the angels and saints as they are deserving of love according to your knowledge of their holiness and the specific ways in which you are indebted to them.

2.   Living and dying in him, with him and through him, make your own, furthermore, the holy intentions of the divine Savior: the glory of God his Father and the salvation and sanctification of others; in a word, the whole reason for which he chose to live and die.

3.   Love God not only in word or in the experience of some tender moment of love but also love God in deed and in truth; with a vibrancy of love that can exclaim with St. Paul, "Who will separate me from the love of my God and of Christ Jesus . . . I am certain that hunger, nakedness, persecution, the sword, and the like will never separate me from it."

4. Do not believe you have arrived at the perfection of holy love of God unless this sacred love will have emptied you of every kind of vanity, sensuality, cowardice, negligence in your pious practices, earthly attachments and affections; in a word, all of nature in order to have you live by the movement of grace and according to the Gospel maxims alone. When it is great, love itself makes us languish on earth and sigh continually for God.

5. Continually ponder this truth: that a holy and exemplary life is incomparably more profitable to the neighbor than eloquence. People are more profoundly moved by a saintly example than by words. Besides, God blesses the works of faithful servants more than those of sinners and the imperfect.

6. Recollect yourself frequently in God and do everything in the presence of God.

+

Spiritual Exercises: Contemplation to Obtain Love

Love ought to manifest itself more by deeds than by words. (SE: #230)

Love consists in a mutual communication between the two persons. That is, the one who loves gives and communicates to the beloved what he or she has, or a part of what one has or can have; and the beloved in return does the same to the lover. Thus, if the one has knowledge, one gives it to the other who does not; and similarly in regard to honors or riches. Each shares with the other. (SE: #231)

I ask for interior knowledge of all the great good I have received, in order that, stirred to profound gratitude, I may become able to love and serve his Divine Majesty in all things. (SE: #233)

Take, Lord and receive all my liberty, my memory, my understanding, and my entire will, all that I have and possess.

You, Lord, have given all that to me. I now give it back to You, Lord. All of it is yours. Dispose of it according to your will. Give me your love and your grace, for that is enough for me. (SE: #234)

+

Maxims of Perfection: Maxims for Obtaining Love

Receive, O my God, my liberty which I offer to Thee, without reserve; accept of my memory, understanding, and will all that I have, all that I am. Thou hast given all to me, I only return them to Thee that Thou mayest dispose of them according to Thy loving and amiable pleasure. (Formulary of Daily Prayers)

Many of these maxims are expressions of apostolic love; others are mixed in content.

1. With preferential love, love God infinitely more than all creatures and see all creatures as infinitely less than God; despise them within this perspective and be content to love God alone and to possess God alone.

2. In honor of the very adorable Holy Spirit who is all love, have for God the more pure and unselfish, the greatest and most perfect love known to you.

3. In honor of the angels and saints, declare firmly that you will try to model yourself on the example of their holy lives and never do anything that contradicts the seeking after the great virtue.

4. Live always not only in the state of grace, since living thus is absolutely necessary for using time profitably, but live, insofar as possible, in the habit and practice of great charity; consecrate to God all your habitual and extraordinary actions with very pure and noble intentions, the principal one of which ought to be a great desire to content and glorify God.

5. In living this love, die to all forms of human respect and to forms of compromise, however, slightly evil, and make open profession of being generously attached to God's service alone and of wanting to tolerate nothing contrary to the respect and worship due his sovereign majesty.

6. Unite all your actions to the merits of the life and death of the Savior Jesus; in general make his divine intentions yours: do them in his name according to the direction of St. Paul; ask for everything through Jesus himself as is the practice of the Church; hope that all you desire to receive from the divine goodness will come from the hands of Jesus who will grant all you desire insofar as it will be more efficacious for your salvation and perfection.

7. See to it that your love for God has the following qualities. Let it be unifying, that is, let it unite you completely and totally to God through the thoughts you think, the affections you feel, and the holiness of your words and works.

8. Love God according to the precept of the Law with your whole heart, your whole soul, and your whole strength.

9. Have for God an expansive love which includes all that love is capable of and all that a heart can love in God and for God; an exalted love full of purpose and ardor, transcending the mass of creatures; a profound heartfelt love which is at your heart's center and cannot be uprooted by any created power.

10. As for your zeal, it will always be proportionate to the love for God in your heart; see that it springs from a great love, and it will be great.

11. To put all this briefly, take as your model in the practice of zeal, (after the Savior Jesus) the great apostle St. Paul; you will learn from him the prudence, sincerity, ardor, unselfishness, constancy and tirelessness of true zeal which you will try to imitate in your works.

12.   Embrace, at least in desire, the conversion and sanctification of a whole world in imitation of apostolic persons and do so with a generous courage which, in the orders of God's good pleasure and of obedience and in the observance of true humility, brings you and urges you to wish to do everything, to undertake everything and to suffer everything in order to glorify God, assist in the salvation and sanctification of those who cost God's dear son everything.

13.   As St. Paul says, let your charity toward your neighbor be patient, beneficent and totally obliging, bearing no trace of bitterness or animosity: of unfavorable or rash judgments, of detraction or the least sign of coldness and or words or gestures in the least way offensive.   In a word, let your charity be filled with the justice of the Gospel and let it fulfill all the demands of the Savior's beautiful maxim: do unto others what you would have others do unto you; and whatever you would not want done to you, do not do unto others.

14. Always have a good opinion of others; always speak well of them; excuse and conceal as best you can all the wrong you might see in them: always be kind to others and never be unkind to anyone.

15.   Always prefer the contentment of others to your own, their wishes to yours; and, whenever there is no danger that God be offended or obviously less honored, be as obliging as you can toward the neighbor; and if, by chance, you have difficulty submitting to the will of others and overcoming your reasonable wishes to follow their whims, in no way let your difficulty become apparent but show a countenance serene and gentle as if you took singular pleasure in what pains you more and causes you more displeasure.

16.   Do whatever you have to for the benefit of the neighbor with the same feeling of devotion as though you were serving Christ Jesus himself or his holy Mother.

17.   Forgive all injuries and, to arrive at a greater perfection of Christian charity, gladly please as far as possible

those who offend you and who displease you most. Do not be content with welcoming opportunities to serve when they arise; carefully and promptly seek them out yourself in order to imitate more perfectly your heavenly Father.

18. Let your love be unselfish and let it always direct you to seek the interests of God's glory alone, even to emptying yourself of your own.

19. Let your love be communicative, obliging you to give yourself unreservedly to God so that you may say in truth the words of the spouse: "I belong to my Beloved, and my Beloved belongs to me."

20. Let your love be active; that is, may it keep loving and urge your heart to keep working for God and for the advancement of God's glory. Then fulfill every demand of this perfect love and at the same time you will have every great virtue and will generously practice them when opportunity arises.

21. Love other Christians with a pure and constant love, an ardent love which, when need be, spends itself for the neighbor as Christ Jesus spent himself wholly for us and for his Church.

22. Love others as yourself; love them as Christ Jesus loved you: love them as true adoptive sons and daughters of God and as members of the Mystical Body whose head is Christ Jesus.

23. When you work for others, have a very unselfish love which expects no reward for its services: presume rather that you will receive only ingratitude, which happens often enough thus in helping the neighbor you will grow accustomed to seeking only the good of serving him and of pleasing God at the same time.

24. Take care to use time fruitfully; it is precious and its loss irreparable.

25. Profit diligently from every opportunity to practice the great virtue of using time well as it presents itself.

26. Strive also wholeheartedly after the peaceful and intimate union with God, very cordial charity and forbearance towards the neighbor, really innocent purity of heart, very perfect fidelity to grace joined to a peaceful death to all natural inclinations, very true humility, simplicity and sincere candor, the obedience of a child who looks for no reason, poverty completely stripped, continual joy of spirit appropriate to your Institute, in a word, attain the pure and perfect love of God which explains all things.

Conclude these devout protestations with a *Veni Creator* in order to ask the Holy Spirit for grace to keep them exactly and to take advantage of them in such a way that, having lived on earth as the saints did, you may share in their glory forever and ever. Amen. God be blessed.

FR. MÉDAILLE ENCOURAGES THE SISTERS OF ST. JOSEPH AND THEIR ASSOCIATES TO PRAY THE *MAXIMS OF PERFECTION* IN THESE WORDS OF EXHORTATION.[76]

EXHORTATION

CONCERNING THE MAXIMS OF PERFECTION FOR THOSE ASPIRING TO THE GREAT VIRTUE

Christian souls, chosen by God to practice perfection in religion or in the world, read the following maxims carefully, meditate upon them frequently, and I hope through divine goodness that they will enlighten you about the great virtue, make known to you in what it consists, and help you to put it into practice. The approbations that two theologians renowned for their profound doctrine and their remarkable holiness have given to this little book make it quite commendable.

Nevertheless, I want to add here the feeling of various persons who read them carefully before they saw the light. They affirmed that, whatever anxiety or disturbing change of heart far removed from Gospel perfection their pride or some alien temptation kindled in them, they fortunately encountered some maxims which dispelled their confusion and their anxiety and which revealed to them the depths and extent of the true virtue. With God's help, you will not profit less from the maxims, my dear reader, if you read and reread them often with profound attention, weighing even the least of the words which comprise them. There are very few which do not have their special meaning and which do not give some new understanding of perfection to the truth that they explain.

Furthermore, take them sometimes as the subject of your daily meditations and when after reflective consideration, you will have penetrated and weighed the meaning of each one of them, reflect on yourself, see how you have practiced its teaching and how you desire to practice it in the future.

And in order to incite you to embrace the practice of them, notice the countless multitude of men and women saints who have lived in the past and who still live in the practice of the virtue which they teach; you will be able to tell yourself the following: "What! can I not do what these have done and what these are doing? Can I not imitate their holiness and follow the example of a perfect life they have given and are giving me?"

Believe, my dear reader, that if you use them in this way, the truths that these few maxims contain will purify your heart, will free it from the affection of all creatures, will enlighten it in order to know the great and true virtue, will make its exercises easier, and provide helps to practice it; in a word, they will fill you with Jesus Christ by stripping you of your self in order to clothe you with his self; and in the fullness of the Holy Spirit they will root you in the possession of a perfect peace, will crown you with merit, and will successfully lead you to the happiness of eternity in order to possess a great glory there. This is the good that I wish for you with all my heart.

+

PART FOUR

THE DAILY EXAMEN
OF
ST. IGNATIUS OF LOYOLA ADAPTED

God's Grandeur

The world is charged with the grandeur of God.
  It will flame out, like shining from shook foil;
  It gathers to a greatness, like the ooze of oil
Crushed.   Why do men then now not reck his rod?
Generations have trod, have trod, have trod;
  And all is seared with trade; bleared, smeared with toil;
  And wears man's smudge and shreds man's smell: the soil
Is bare now, nor can foot feel, being shod.
And for all this, nature is never spent;
  There lives the dearest freshness deep down things;
And though the last lights off the black West went
  Oh, morning, at the brown brink eastward springs--
Because the Holy Ghost over the bent
  World broods with warm breast and with ah! bright wings.[77]

Gerard Manley Hopkins

THE DAILY EXAMEN
OF
ST. IGNATIUS OF LOYOLA ADAPTED
PRAYER FOR FINDING GOD IN ALL THINGS[78]

What Is the Daily Examen?

The examen is spiritual exercise--a period of prayer during which time I review my daily life. I reflect on the seeking and finding of God in my daily experience. God is as present to me as I am to myself. I live in the ordinary but am always being affected by the extraordinary. God's power is always at work in me. God's eternal vision is at work in the temporal.

"I am with you all days even to the end of the world." (Matt. 28:20)

Like personal prayer, the daily examen is union with God in restful prayer. Taking about fifteen minutes to complete, it should be done in the middle and at the end of the day. It roots me in Christ. I die to selfishness and put on Christ. I am transformed into God's image and likeness.

"God became one of us that we might become like God."
Early Fathers

The daily examen is important in personal and communal discernment, i.e., in the making of right choices at the level of faith. The daily examen provides the opportunity for evaluating my activities, i.e., solitude with God and with myself, time with others. It is a necessity for the active and mobile Christian. From moment to moment, demands are made on my time and energy, patience and wisdom. The sincerity of my Christian love is tested every hour of the day.

The daily examen keeps me steady and poised before all created things. It trains me to listen to the Spirit and to find God at work in the sacrament of the present moment. My life becomes the raw material for holiness.
"We are God's work of art created in Christ Jesus to live the good life as he meant us to live it from the beginning." (Eph. 2:10)

SOME REFLECTIONS ON THE DAILY EXAMEN

"Consider the end of our studies. The scholastics can hardly give themselves to prolonged meditations. Over and above the spiritual exercises assigned for their perfection, namely daily Mass, an hour for vocal prayer and examen of conscience, weekly confession and communion, they should practice the seeking of God in all things, in their conversations, their walks, in all that they see, taste, hear, understand, in all their actions, since His Divine Majesty is truly in all things by His presence, power and essence . . . this method is an excellent exercise to prepare us for great visitations of our Lord.[79]

"Desire the perfection suitable to the three powers of your soul: for the memory, a forgetfulness of all things, even of self, in order to remember God alone; for the seeing of God in all things, the glory, the power, the providence, the mercy of God; for the will, the liberty of approaching God, of loving God and of embracing all the orders of God's providence with all the affection of your soul."[80]

"Don't skip the examen. Have a definite time for doing it. Human nature must serve you."

"We must habitually pray over our thoughts, our speech, opinions, aspirations, desires, decisions, over our physical, spiritual, material and mental needs, over our vows and our state of calling so that we may better discern the will of God, respect our neighbor, and properly understand their lives, actions, and efforts in the spirit of charity."

"It is the mystics who are in closest touch with reality because they are at one with it. They can find and touch God at any given moment."[81]

+

Spiritual Exercises: A Method for Making the General Examination of Conscience. It contains five points. (SE: #43)

THE FIRST POINT is to give thanks to God our Lord for the benefits I have received from him.

THE SECOND is to ask grace to know my sins and rid myself of them.

THE THIRD is to ask an account of my soul from the hour or rising to the present examen, hour by hour or period by period; first as to thoughts, then words, then deeds, in the same order as was given for the particular examen [SE: #25: exacting an account of oneself with regard to the particular matter one has decided to take for correction and improvement.]

THE FOURTH is to ask pardon of God our Lord for my faults.

THE FIFTH is to resolve, with his grace, to amend them. Close with an Our Father. (SE: #43)

+

THE DAILY EXAMEN PROPER

1. GRATITUDE. I thank God for having created me, for showering so many gifts on me, for the experience of life itself.
"O Lord, you have done marvels for me; holy is your name." (Lk. 1:46-47)
"Without me you can do nothing." (Jn. 15:5)
". . . You have given all to me. I now return it to you to be used simply as you wish." Suscipe of St. Ignatius of Loyola

2. ASK THE HOLY SPIRIT FOR THE GRACE OF SELF-KNOWLEDGE. Ask for God's viewpoint in order to see the day according to God's active and permissive will.
"Speak Lord, your servant is listening." (1 Sam. 3:10).
"The Holy Spirit whom the Father will send in my name will teach you everything and remind you of all I have said." (Jn. 14:26)
"Heavenly Father, give me the Spirit through Jesus your Son." (Bl. Peter Favre, S.J.)
"Do you not understand that you are God's temple, and that God's Spirit dwells in you?" (1 Cor. 3:16)

3. PRELIMINARY REFLECTIONS: Was today generally a "good" or "bad" day? Recall the day's experiences. *(At the time of examen, it may prove helpful to keep a written record of the morning and afternoon activities in a notebook from the hour of rising.)*

Were there any images which made a deep impression on me, i.e., a personal meeting, a conversation whose emotional overtones I vividly recall? Images or emotions of joy, quiet satisfaction, peace or of anger, frustration, resentment, stress, tension?
What were my first and basic impulses resulting from these deep impressions? The basic impulses of each day can be described as those immediate reactions or responses which evoke consolation or desolation. In the final analysis, "one must be . . . led into consolation because this is the characteristic of the good spirit by whom we wish to be guided."[82]

Words associated with consolation: ability to communicate, clarity, contentment, ease, energy, equanimity, generosity, flexibility, inner quiet, insight, joy, patience, peace, self-control, understanding, unselfishness.

Words associated with desolation: agitation, anxiety, bad temper, bitterness, brooding, confusion, disorder, distaste, distraction, ennui, grief, hurt, inner noise, rigidity, sadness, self-indulgence.[83]

4. Do I KNOW MY MAIN WEAKNESS? A basic fault, quality or attachment can trigger a series of faults and can affect my relationship with God, with myself, with others, and in dealing with circumstances in which I find myself.

Am I given to extremes, to too much or too little? Do I seek God's will instead of my own? Am I materialistic? Am I inordinately attached to persons, places, things? Do I tend to pamper my body, to overstimulate my senses? Am I at the core an angry, envious or anxious person? Noisy or critical? Pessimistic, slothful? Am I a workaholic, a perfectionist? What keeps me from living as a happy person?

"My sin is always before me." (Ps. 51:3)

5. I WILL RECALL (A) TIME WITH GOD, (B) TIME WITH MYSELF, (C) TIME WITH OTHERS, (D) CIRCUMSTANCES IN WHICH I FOUND MYSELF. How did my basic fault affect my presence and/or responses to:

GOD: Did I pray today? If not, do I have a valid reason? What was the quality of my personal prayer, liturgical prayer, my spiritual reading? Did my basic fault enter my prayer? Is prayer a time of loving union with Love alone? Did I listen to the inner promptings of the Spirit?

"Be still and know that I am God." (Ps. 46:10)

SELF: Am I a quiet person from within and without? Does my speech come from the depths of silence? "The Spirit of God has made his home in [me] . . . the temple of God is sacred, and [I] am that temple?" (Rom. 8:9, 1 Cor. 3:17) What I say to myself is often more important than what I say to others. Did I work peacefully or in agitation? Did I pause for leisure time? Did I develop my mind and heart, my sense of the beautiful all to the greater glory of God? Did I watch too much TV?

How does my basic fault control me? Am I aware that time is God's time? The kingdom of God is among us. Did I try to show forth the trinitarian God dwelling within me? Did I try to bring Christ's light to my world today? Can I bravely bear suffering, forbidding it to enter the higher part of my spirit wherein abides the Spirit of peace? Have I allowed suffering to sour my life? Is there a lack of sweetness in my life?

"I cannot understand my own behavior. I fail to carry out the things I want to do, and I find myself doing the very things I hate." (Rom. 7:15)

OTHERS: Did I spend myself for others today? Love is proved in deeds. Did I seek and find God in others? Did I treat others as though they are temples of God? How was I affected by others--those with whom I work and live? Is there darkness in my human relationships?

How much tolerance do I have for weakness in others? Am I fussy, rigid, stiff, intolerant of others' faults? If so, why?

Do I value the silence of charity and confidentiality?

"I give you a new commandment: love one another just as I have loved you." (Jn. 13:34)

CIRCUMSTANCES: Do I feel anger or bitterness at the circumstances in which I find myself? Why? How did I respond to the events of today, to those situations over which I had no control? Did I deal with conflict serenely and creatively?

Did I look for God in and through difficult experiences? The situations in which I find myself are God's will for me. Nothing happens by accident.

"Give us joy to balance our affliction for the years when we knew evil." (Ps. 90:15)

6. SORROW FOR MY FAULTS. If today's experiences were difficult, let them be seen in the light of what the Lord Jesus suffered for me. He became weakness; he has absorbed my weakness.

"Come to me, all you who labor and are overburdened, and I

84

will give you rest. Shoulder my yoke and learn from me, for I am gentle and humble of heart, and you will find rest for your souls. Yes, my yoke is easy and my burden light." (Matt. 11:28-30)

"I will turn their mourning into joy, I will console and gladden them after their sorrows." (Jer. 31:14)

"For you are my rock, my fortress; for the sake of your name, guide me, lead me! (Ps. 31:3)

7. A RESOLVE TO MAKE A FRESH START. Do not brood over the past. Live in the sacrament of the present moment. With a grateful heart, thank God for the blessings and favors received today.

"Give me only your love and your grace; it is all I need." Suscipe of St. Ignatius of Loyola

"O Lord, you have done marvels for me; holy is your name." (Lk. 1:46-47)

"God grant me serenity to accept the things I cannot change, courage to change the things I can and wisdom to know the difference." The Serenity Prayer

"Where sin did abound, grace did more abound." (Rom. 5: 21)

8. PRAYER: the Lord's Prayer, Mary's Magnificat, Anima Christi, the Jesus Prayer or a favorite psalm.

MARY'S MAGNIFICAT

My soul proclaims the greatness of the Lord,
and my spirit exults in God my savior;
because he has looked upon his lowly handmaid.
Yes, from this day forward all generations will call me blessed,
for the Almighty has done great things for me.
Holy is his name,
and his mercy reaches from age to age for those who fear him.
He has shown the power of his arm,
He has routed the proud of heart.
He has pulled down the princes from their thrones and exalted the lowly.
The hungry he has filled with good things, the rich sent empty away.
He has come to the help of Israel his servant, mindful of his mercy
—according to the promise he made to our ancestors--
of his mercy to Abraham and to his descendants for ever.

ANIMA CHRISTI

Soul of Christ, sanctify me.
Body of Christ, save me.
Blood of Christ, inebriate me,.
Water from the side of Christ, wash me
Passion of Christ, strengthen me.
O good Jesus, hear me.
Within thy wounds, hide me.
Suffer me not to be separated from thee.
From the malignant enemy, defend me.
In the hour of my death, call me.
And bid me come to thee,
That with thy saints I may praise thee
Forever and ever. Amen

THE JESUS PRAYER

Jesus, Son of David, have mercy on me, a sinner.

As kingfishers catch fire, dragonflies dráw fláme

. . . The just man justices;
Kéeps gráce; that keeps all his going graces;
Acts in God's eye what in God's eye he is--
Chríst—for Christ plays in ten thousand places,
Lovely in limbs, and lovely in eyes not his
To the Father through the features of men's faces.

Gerard Manley Hopkins, S.J.

PART FIVE

ST. JOSEPH

Her husband Joseph,
being a righteous man and unwilling to expose her to public disgrace,
planned to dismiss her quietly.

But just when he had resolved to do this,
an angel of the Lord appeared to him in a dream and said:

"Joseph, son of David,
do not be afraid
to take Mary as your wife,
for the child conceived in her
is from the Holy Spirit." (Mt. 1:19-20)

WHY THE NAME 'SISTERS OF ST. JOSEPH'?

WHY DID FR. MÉDAILLE DEDICATE THE INSTITUTE TO ST. JOSEPH? Could he not have named the Institute after the Holy Trinity or the Holy Family? Why the dedication to St. Joseph? There may have been a pragmatic reason for naming the 'institute' after St. Joseph: the early association ministered in the hospital named "St. Joseph." Under Joseph's watchful guidance as well as Mary's, Jesus grew in wisdom, in stature and in favor with God. He grew to perfect maturity and manhood. Thus, dedication of an institute to St. Joseph would have been perfectly acceptable. Fr. Médaille reinforces this thought:

> "Firmly honor St. Joseph [so] that you will serve and love Jesus and Mary wholeheartedly as he served and loved them, and that when you serve the neighbor, you will do so in Joseph's spirit of humility, gentleness and charity."

Like her patron, the Sister of St. Joseph centers her life of prayer, her entire life, on Jesus "the image of the unseen God" (Col. 1: 15) and on his Mother, who fulfills a central role in the economy of redemption. The apostolic life of the Sister of St. Joseph is characterized by humility and cordial charity. She allows God to work through her talents which are used under the influence of grace. In this posture are they not rendered all the more attractive? The Sister of St. Joseph approaches the world as sacramental mystery. Fr. Médaille would liken this attitude to humility, gentleness and charity.

St. Teresa of Avila (1515-1582) had great devotion to St. Joseph. As a Doctor of the Church and a special patron on whose feast Sisters of St. Joseph celebrate Founder's Day, the great saint writes:

I took for my advocate and lord the glorious St. Joseph and earnestly recommended myself to him. I saw clearly that as in this need so in other greater ones concerning honor and loss of soul, this father and lord of mine came to my rescue in better ways than I knew how to ask for. I don't recall up to this day ever having petitioned him for anything he failed to grant. It is an amazing thing the great many favors God has granted me through the mediation of this blessed saint, the dangers I was freed from both of body and soul. For with other saints, it seems the Lord has given them grace to be of help in one need, whereas with this glorious saint I have experience that he helps in all our needs and that the Lord wants us to understand that just as He was subject to St. Joseph on earth--for since bearing the title of father, being the Lord's tutor, Joseph could give the Child commands--so in heaven God does whatever he commands.[84]

Sr. Emily Joseph offers her own reflection on St. Joseph:

Joseph, 'of the house and family of David' was chosen by Bishop de Maupas and Jean-Pierre Médaille as patron of the congregation they founded in 1650. Sisters of St. Joseph see their patron as one who was 'all things to all men.'

In symbol, the lily signifies that Joseph is the virgin father of the Son of God; the T-square identifies him as St. Joseph the Worker. Yet the glory of this saint does not depend on achievements which can be denoted by exterior signs. In the case of St. Joseph no episcopal or regal robes, no insignia distinguished him; he carried no crusader's cross nor did he meet a martyr's death. What set St. Joseph apart, what elevated him to the heights of sanctity that we cannot conceive was his love of God, his absolute trust.

In hours of silent contemplation, there had been revealed to him his special relationship with each of the Three Divine Persons: from among all men he had been selected to be the shadow of the Eternal Father; by his marriage with Mary, he became the legal father of the Son of God; by the overshadowing of the Holy Spirit, the Word became incarnate in his beloved spouse. These truths, too sacred to find expression in words, St. Joseph stored in the recesses of his soul and there pondered in silent prayer.

In their patron, Sisters of St. Joseph find an ideal model for the 'contemplation-in-action' vocation that is theirs. In contemplation they come to know themselves as temples of the Holy Spirit upon whom they endeavor to concentrate all power of their soul in holy adoration. In their active apostolates they exert themselves in intimacy with Christ beside whom St. Joseph toiled day after day at the carpenter's bench.

Well may the Sister of St. Joseph pray to her patron: 'Help me, St. Joseph, to fulfill as you did the vocation in life to which God has called me. Intercede for me that like you, I may keep my hope fixed unchangeably on Christ and in loving trust, pray and work *ad maiorem Dei gloriam.'*"[85]

In the 1950's a set of scriptural meditations in honor of St. Joseph was arranged by a Sister of St. Joseph as outlined by Fr. Louis Lallemant, S.J.[86] The novena has come to be known as the scriptural Four-point Novena to St. Joseph. This novena is provided on the next page.[87]

NOVENA TO ST. JOSEPH
by
Fr. Louis Lallemant, S.J.

THE SCRIPTURAL NOVENA TO ST. JOSEPH CONSISTS IN TURNING TO ST. Joseph four times a day (it does not matter where or when) and honoring him in the four points of:

1. HIS FIDELITY TO GRACE: Think of this for a minute, thank God and ask through St. Joseph to be faithful to grace.

2. HIS FIDELITY TO THE INTERIOR LIFE: Think, thank God, and ask.

3. HIS LOVE OF OUR BLESSED LADY: Think, thank God, and ask.

4. HIS LOVE OF THE HOLY CHILD: Think, thank God, and ask.

Explanation of the points to be considered:

1. FIDELITY TO GRACE. By this is meant St. Joseph's consciousness of God's life within him and his desire to increase that life. It also refers to his cooperation with all the graces that God sent to him constantly, that is, graces which enlightened his mind and moved his will to do good and it avoid evil.

2. FIDELITY TO THE INTERIOR LIFE. The interior life is the life of the spirit, the life of God within, the awareness of God and devotion to duty for the greater honor and glory of God; it embraces also the practice of virtue which is associated with living a life of prayer, the continual remembrance of the presence of God, acceptance of God's will, humility of heart, the spirit of sacrifice and life.

3. LOVE OF OUR LADY. It means thinking about the devotion of St. Joseph to Mary and how he was chosen by her as her spouse; how he was told by God's messenger of the mystery of her Divine Motherhood. St. Joseph was the protector of Mary and the head of the Holy Family. He realized better than anyone else her part in the Divine Plan for our salvation. His natural love for her was increased and strengthened and perfected by his supernatural love and devotion to her.

4. LOVE OF THE CHRIST CHILD. St. Joseph was told that the Christ Child was the Son of God and the Savior of the world. He was mindful of the duty which was his of protecting and caring for the Infant Savior. His faith in Christ was manifested in the many trials and difficulties that St. Joseph experienced. His love for Jesus was deep and genuine and profound. It was a love that revealed itself not only in word but especially in service.

(The four points are to be taken for each meditation. This four-point novena has been found to be so efficacious that one is advised to be sure that one really wants what one asks for. To make the minute meditations as suggested by the points of the Novena, the scriptural events from the life of St. Joseph are used as the topic for each of the four points for each day).

FIRST DAY

St. Joseph's Great Trial
(Matt. 1: 18, 19)

Joseph had no knowledge of Mary's Divine Motherhood, and he was perplexed and uncertain. He did not know what to do about his proposed marriage . Being "a just man," he did not wish to turn Mary over to the Law or to exposes her for reproach. He decided to put her away quietly. He was convinced of her innocence, but he had no way of proving it to himself. *(Think, thank God, and ask).*

SECOND DAY

Message of the Angel to Joseph
Concerning Mary's Innocence
(Matt. 1: 20-25)

The angel said to him, "Fear not, Joseph, son of David, to take to yourself Mary your wife, for that which is begotten of her is of the Holy Spirit." Further, it was made known to him that the Child to be born of Mary was to be named Jesus by Joseph, because he would save his people from their sins. *(Think, thank God, and ask).*

THIRD DAY

The Census
(Luke 2: 1-3)

Picture St. Joseph and Mary living quietly in Nazareth expecting the birth of the Christ Child. Suddenly a notice is received that a census is to be taken, and everyone must return to his own city to be enrolled. This means great hardship to Joseph and to Mary who was with Child. Nevertheless, Joseph and Mary started out on the long journey to Bethlehem despite the hardships and difficulties they knew would be theirs. *(Think, thank God, and ask).*

FOURTH DAY

Joseph and the Birth of Christ
(Luke 2: 4-7)

Consider St. Joseph's inability to find a place of lodging, the need of going to a cave outside of the town, then the birth of the Christ Child. It is very easy to see the four points of the meditation in this wonderful scene, picturing Joseph's love and devotion as he worships the Christ Child with Mary his mother beside him. *(Think, thank God, and ask).*

FIFTH DAY

Joseph and the Shepherds
and the Magi
(Luke 2: 8-20; Matt. 2: 1-12)

See the shepherds hastening to Bethlehem to see the Christ Child and to tell the message of the angels, "Glory to God in the highest, and on earth peace to men of good will." It is easy to imagine the happiness of these simple shepherds, their joy and their exultation as they worship the new born King. With the visit of the shepherds can be associated the visit of the Magi, Wise Men from the east, who have come to adore the Christ Child and to offer him the precious gifts of gold, frankincense and myrrh. *(Think, thank God, and ask)*.

SIXTH DAY

Joseph and the Presentation of the
Child Jesus in the Temple
(Luke 2: 22:38)

Call to mind the strong St. Joseph carrying the Christ Child to the crowded Temple where Mary takes the Divine Infant and presents him to the priest. Joseph realizes that Jesus is the Light of the world, and that this is the initial offering of Christ in his life of sacrifice. He hears too, with great sorrow, the words of Simeon to Mary, ". . . and your own soul a sword shall pierce." *(Think, thank God, and ask)*.

SEVENTH DAY
Joseph and the Flight into Egypt
(Matt. 2: 13-15; 19-21)

Reflect on the anxiety of St. Joseph as he is told by an angel to take Mary and the Child and flee into Egypt. Joseph obeys at once, and the Holy Family departs under the cover of night. The journey is long, over four hundred miles, and difficult. For almost two years the Holy Family must remain in Egypt surrounded by strangers and in great sorrow. *(Think, thank God, and ask)*.

EIGHTH DAY

Joseph and the Loss of the
Christ Child in the Temple
(Luke 2: 41-50)

The natural anxiety of St. Joseph for the Christ Child, when it is discovered that he is not with the friends of the Holy Family can hardly be described. Frantically Joseph and Mary look for him and after three days, they find him in the temple talking to the doctors of the Law and instructing them. Mary and Joseph rejoice to find Jesus, but they hear from his lips the mysterious words, "Did you not know that I must be about my Father's business." *(Think, thank God, and ask)*.

NINTH DAY

The Death of St. Joseph

Sacred Scripture says nothing about the death of St. Joseph and we must supply what took place as best we can. See St. Joseph on his death bed realizing the graces which God gave him during his life, fully conscious of the life of God within him and the life of virtue he has lived. He has lived life to the full with the Incarnate Word, the God-Man and the Mother of God. He could ask for no more in his earthly sojourn. One can presume that Jesus and Mary were at his death bed and that they comforted him, consoled him and reassured him. St. Joseph is the patron of a happy death because he died in the presence of Jesus and Mary. *(Think, thank God, and ask)*.

96

EPILOGUE

From the earliest foundations, the Sisters of St. Joseph have labored in the vinyard as women for others. We entered the "Congregation of the Great Love of God" with open hearts not knowing what the future would hold. We gave ourselves unreservedly to God who called us into existence and who continues to be faithful to us.

With the advent of a new century, the Sister of St. Joseph must once again ask herself: What will I do for Christ, for his Body--the People of God? Like the holy men and women of scripture, like Mary and Joseph, like Ignatius, Teresa, and Jean-Pierre, we have been set apart, chosen for service to others. As consecrated religious women, we belong to God alone and not to ourselves or to the world. We are God's lovers in the market place. We are lovers in action for love begets love-energy.

Life in the whole Christ leads us to the mountain top of prayer where we see, and listen and are prompted by the triune God to serve *ad maiorem Dei gloriam*. The demands of the market place test the mettle of our prayer, and discipleship inevitably brings us face to face with the cross. It must be so if we are to follow in the footsteps of Mary and Joseph who began to share in their Son's Passion even on their difficult journey to Bethlehem prior to his birth. But surely they were among the first to know the joy of their Son's Resurrection.

Tomorrow may surprise and even confuse us. The God of order and of consolation will be with us as we love God into the world. And now the Spirit beckons us: Return to the fountainhead, the source of your vitality! Let us seek and find God in all our waking hours as we proclaim the great love of God for all to see *ad maiorem Dei gloriam*. I would like to bring this labor of love to a close with Eileen Lomasney's poem "Limbo." It is a fitting tribute to St. Joseph our very own Patron and Patron of the Universal Church . . . .

Limbo

The ancient greyness shifted
Suddenly and thinned
Like mist upon the moors
Before a wind.
An old, old prophet lifted
A shining face and said:
"He will be coming soon.
The Son of God is dead;
He died this afternoon."

A murmurous excitement stirred
All souls.
They wondered if they dreamed--
Save one old man who seemed
Not even to have heard.

And Moses standing.
Hushed them all to ask
If any had a welcome song prepared.
If not, would David take the task?
And if they cared
Could not the three young children sing
The Benedicite, the canticle of praise
They made when God kept them from perishing
In the fiery blaze?

A breath of spring surprised them,
Stilling Moses' words.
No one could speak, remembering
The first fresh flowers,
The little singing birds.
Still others thought of fields new ploughed
Or apple trees
All blossom-boughed.
Or some, the way a dried bed fills
With water
Laughing down green hills.

The fisherfolk dreamed of the foam
On bright blue seas.
The one old man who had not stirred
Remembered home.

And there He was.
Splendid as the morning sun and fair
As only God is fair.
And they, confused with joy,
Knelt to adore
Seeing that He wore
Five crimson stars
He never had before.

No canticle at all was sung.
None toned a psalm, or raised a greeting song.
A silent man alone
Of all that throng
Found tongue--
Not any other.
Close to His heart
When the embrace was done,
Old Joseph said,
"How is Your Mother,
How is Your Mother, Son?"[88]

Eileen Lomasney, C.S.J.

amdg

ENDNOTES

1. Jean-Pierre Médaille, S.J., *Maximes de Perfection*, edited by M. Nepper, S.J., Lyons: Roudil Frères, 3 Quai A-Lassagne, 1962, quoted in Médaille Committee, "The Spirituality of Reverend Jean-Pierre Médaille, S.J., (New Orleans, 1967) 3.

2. Ibid., *Maxims of Perfection*, translated and commissioned by the Federation, Sisters of St. Joseph, U.S.A. . . . under the direction of M. Nepper, S.J. (Erie, PA: McCarty Printing Corp., 1978) Foreword, iii.

3. David J. Nygren and Miriam D. Ukeritis, "The Religious Life Futures Project: Executive Summary," *Review for Religious*, 52/1 (January-February) 25.

4. Sisters of St. Joseph, *A Story with an Endless Beginning* (Paris: Caldirola, Dolfy, 1987).

5. *A Hopkins Reader*, revised and enlarged edition, edited with an introduction by John Pick, (Garden City, NY: Image Books, 1966): 67.

6. In the same Toulouse province of Jesuits there was another Médaille named Pierre who wrote *Méditations sur les Evangiles de l'année.*

7. Anne Bernice Hennessey, C.S.J.: "The Influence of Ignatian Spirituality on the Primitive Documents of the Sisters of St. Joseph," (M.A. thesis, 1983) 27, n. 18.

8. Bangert narrates: "For nearly four decades after Régis' death, Jean-Paul Médaille, who was formed in the saint's [Ignatius'] methods, carried on the labor of christian instruction in the hamlets and villages of Auvergne, Velay and Languedoc. He also assisted in the creation of the Congregation of the Sisters of St. Joseph, who made the rule of Saint Ignatius the basis of their institute. See William V. Bangert, S.J., *A History of the Society of Jesus*, (St. Louis: The Institute of Jesuit Sources, 1972) 211.

9. Marius Nepper, S.J., *Origins of the Sisters of St. Joseph*, trans. U.S. Federation Research team (Erie, PA: Villa Maria College, 1969) 4-6, quoted in Hennessey, "The Influence of Ignatian Spirituality," 4.

10. This mission may have established contact between some pious women and Fr. Médaille. Roman records state that he did not inform the General of the Society of Jesus of his assocations with the women of Le Puy.

Letters from Rome are uneasy as to the kind of association he had established with these women.

11. *Primitive Constitutions* and Le Puy Archive, quoted in the *Constitutions of the Sisters of St. Joseph,* 27. *Cassell's Latin Dictionary* offers the Ciceronian meaning of 'bilious' as 'melancholy' while *The American College Dictionary* and *The Oxford English Dictionary* give meanings such as: peevish, testy, cross (*ACD*) and choleric, wrathful, peevish,. ill-tempered (*OED*).

12. Nepper, S.J., *Origins of the Sisters of St. Joseph,* quoted in Hennessey, "The Influence of Ignatian Spirituality," 4.

13. Hennessey, "The Influence of Ignatian Spirituality," 11.

14. Ibid., 91.

15. Composed on the occasion of the Sesquicentennial of the Sisters of St. Joseph of Carondelet, 1836-1986.

16. Although documents use "founder/founders" for seven different people in Le Puy alone, it was Fr. Médaille who recognized a special charism in the women who eventually became known as *"les filles de St. Joseph."*

17. The thirteen thousand Sisters of St. Joseph in the United States form part of a world-wide body of twenty-five thousand Sisters of St. Joseph in four Federations: the French, the Canadian, the Italian and the United States Federations." Sisters of St. Joseph, *A Story with an Endless Beginning,* VI.

18. Médaille, S.J., *Maximes de Perfection,* 3.

19. Médaille Committee, "The Spirituality of Reverend Jean-Pierre Médaille, S.J." (New Orleans, 1967) 2-3.

20. Sisters of St. Joseph, *A Story with an Endless Beginning,* 18.

21. Ibid.

22. *St. Ignatius' Own Story,* trans. by William J. Young, S.J. (Henry Regnery Co., 1956) 103.

23. Pierre Wolf, S.J., "Keynote Address to Sisters of St. Joseph, Albany Province (Latham, NY: April 16, 1983) 1-2.

24. Prior to the eighteenth century, the word "religious" was identified with cloistered religious women.

25. George E. Ganss, S.J., "Editor's Foreword in David L. Fleming, S.J., *The Spiritual Exercises of St. Ignatius: A Literal Translation and a Contemporary Reading*, (St. Louis: The Institute of Jesuit Sources, 1970) xiii.

26. *The Spiritual Exercises of St. Ignatius of Loyola*, A New Translation by Thomas Corbishley, S.J. (London: Burns and Oates, 1963) 9.

27. Most apostolic orders and congregations founded since 1600 have been heavily influenced by Ignatian spirituality.

28. John C. Futrell, S.J., "Discovering the Founder's Charism," *The Way Supplement* 64 (Autumn, 1971) 63.

29. Cheslyn Jones, Geoffrey Wainwright, Edward, Yarnold, S.J., eds., *The Study of Spirituality*, (New York & Oxford: Oxford University Press, 1986) 361.

30. *The Autobiography of Ignatius of Loyola* in *The Classics of Western Spirituality*, George E. Ganss, S.J., ed. (New York & Mahwah: Paulist Press, 1990) 79-80.

31. Hugo Rahner, S.J., *Ignatius the Theologian*, translated by Michael Barry (New York: Herder and Herder, 1968) 3.

32. Ibid.

33. Hennessey, "The Influence of Ignatian Spirituality," 105, 115, 126.

34. Rahner, *Ignatius the Theologian*, 9.

35. Ibid., 12.

36. *Constitution of the Sisters of Saint Joseph* (Brentwood, NY: N.P) 4.

37. Hennessy, "The Influence of Ignatian Spirituality," 103.

38. Ibid., 84.

39. When the Federation Team translated and wrote this Statement in this form, the spacing, lines, etc. were part of the message, i.e., the one sentence with no break thus conveying the one flow of grace.

40. Cheslyn Jones, *The Study of Spirituality*, 361.

41. St. Francis de Sales' *Introduction to the Devout Life* is based on the schema and content of the *Spiritual Exercises*. In fact, many passages paraphrase those of the *Exercises*. The spiritual influence of Bishop de Maupas on the early founding shows that he too "was a recipient of this [Ignatian] influence as a result of his Jesuit education and his Jesuit spiritual directors." See Hennessey, "The Influence of Ignatian Spirituality," 22.

42. Another mystic and poet, St. John of the Cross (1542-1591) is influenced in his writings by the *Spiritual Exercises of St. Ignatius*. St. John of the Cross attended Jesuit college (1559-1563) where he "received a solid formation in the humanities." See *The Collected Works of St. John of the Cross*, translated by Kieran Kavanaugh, O.C.D. and Otilio Rodriguez, O.C.D. (Washington DC: ICS Publications, 1973) 16.

43. Hennessy, "The Influence of Ignatian Spirituality," 17.

44. St. Ignatius of Loyola, *The Constitutions of the Society of Jesus*, translated, with an introduction and a commentary by George E. Ganss, S.J. (St. Louis, MO: The Institute of Jesuit Sources, 1970) 263.

45. See Note 10.

46. "Soeurs de St. Joseph de Chambéry en Russie, 1863-1922," (mai-juin 1988) commemorating the millennium of the baptism of 'Russia.'

47. Mary Milligan, "What Is an 'Ignatian Congregation'?" *The Way Supplement* 70 (Spring 1991) 42.

48. Hennessey, "The Influence of Ignatian Spirituality," 10.

49. Ibid., 98.

50. Milligan, "What Is an 'Ignatian Congregation'?" 40-50.

51. Ibid., 41-50.

52. Ibid., 41.

53. St. Ignatius of Loyola, *The Constitutions of the Society of Jesus*, 75-118.

54. *Perfectae caritatis*, Decree on the Adaptation and Renewal of the Religious Life, October 28, 1965, Austin Flannery, ed., *Vatican Council II* New Revised Edition (Northport, NY: Costello Publishing Company, 1992) 627.

55. St. Ignatius of Loyola, *The Spiritual Exercises,* #21 and Jean-Pierre Médaille, *Maxims of Perfection,* Opening Page.

56. Karl Rahner, *Theological Investigations* VII: 15 quoted in Harvey D. Egan, S.J., "Karl Rahner: Theologian of the *Spiritual Exercises,*" *Thought* LXVII/266 (September 1992) 261., n. 3.

57. Michael J. Buckley, S.J. "Mission in Companionship: of Jesuit Community and Communion," *Studies in the Spirituality of Jesuits,* II/4: 15 quoted in George A. Aschenbrenner, S.J. "Jesuit Qualities of Missionary Availability and Finding God in All Things," *Review for Religious,* 49/4 (July/August 1990) 495.

58. Josef Stierli, S.J., "Ignatian Prayer: Seeking God in All Things," in *Ignatius of Loyola: His Personality and Spiritual Heritage,* Friedrich Wulf, S.J., ed. (St. Louis, MO: The Institute of Jesuit Sources, 1977) 139.

59. *New Catholic Encyclopedia,* s.v., "Spiritual Exercises," by J. Lewis, 578-582.

60. Ganss, *Ignatius of Loyola* in *The Classics of Western Spirituality,* 58-59.

61. Ibid., 122.

62. Ibid., 389

63. Hennessey, "The Influence of Ignatian Spirituality," 101. The first *"filles de St. Joseph"* practiced poverty, chastity and obedience with as much perfection as if they had vowed them.

64. Ibid., 59.

65. For example: "The true motto of a person whom God mercifully chooses to use for his glory or on whom God showers loving blessings should be that of St. Paul: 'I am what I am by the grace of my God,' or that of St. Teresa after the Royal Prophet: 'I will forever sing the mercies of God.'"
"Empty yourself constantly in honor of the Incarnate Word who lovingly emptied himself for you. In this self-emptying, profess the most sincere and profound humility that you come to know."

66. For example: "Desire no praise or reward whatsoever for your good works in this life and you will have a more perfect and great reward in eternity. Oh, how meaningless esteem and reward for our actions in this world lessen their merit in the other."
"Always have a good opinion of others; always speak well of them, and

excuse and conceal as best you can all the wrong you might see in them: always be kind to others and never unkind to anyone."

67. For example: "Always be serious-minded in your relationship with others; let it be a pleasant and gracious seriousness in which there is neither unrestraint not too much constraint, and seek relaxation, as indeed you should, at the proper time. The bow that is always taut will soon snap."
"Never complain except about yourself; always accuse yourself and excuse others."

68. For example: "Desire little in this world, and be not overeager for what you may desire!"
"In living your life have only one desire: to be and to become the person God wills you to be in nature, in grace, in glory for time and for eternity."

69. *Maxims of Perfection*, 21.

70. Hennessey, "The Influence of Ignatian Spirituality," 99.

71. Ibid., 100.

72. Apart from some minor changes, the translation used in this work is the one which was commissioned by the Federation. It was made in 1978 by the Intercongregational Research Team under the direction of M. Nepper, S.J.

73. The translation of the *Spiritual Exercises* used in this part is that of George E. Ganss, S.J., *The Classics of Western Spirituality*, 113-214.

74. Although the *'magis'* maxims have been placed at the beginning of the Second Week, the comparative degree is found throughout the maxims.

75. The maxims beginning with the word "declare" have a global perspective.

76. Médaille, *Maxims of Perfection*, Foreword, iii.

77. Gerard Manley Hopkins, "God's Grandeur," *A Hopkins Reader*, 47.

78. Part Four has been published separately as a leaflet. Joan L. Roccasalvo, C.S.J. *The Daily Examen of St. Ignatius of Loyola: Prayer for Finding God in All Things* (Brentwood, NY: 1989, 1991, 1993).

79. *St. Ignatius' Own Story*, 103.

80. A maxim of perfection.

81. Walter J. Ciszek, S.J., Retreat Notes.

82. Brian O'Leary, S.J., *The Discernment of Spirits in the Memoriale of Blessed Peter Favre* in *The Way*, Supplement, 35 (1979) 82.

83. Ibid., 111-123.

84. *The Book of Her Life* in *The Collected Works of St. Teresa of Avila*, Volume One, Translated by Kieran Kavanaugh, O.C.D. and Otilio Rodriguez, O.C.D. (Washington, D.C.: ICS Publications, 1976): 53.

85. An excerpt from Sister Emily Joseph, C.S.J., *Reflecting on Saint Joseph*, (St. Anthony Guild Press, 1959) 57-59.

86. *The Spiritual Doctrine of Father Louis Lallemant of the Society of Jesus*, Alan G. McDougall, ed., (Westminster, MD: The Newman Book Shop, 1946) 10-12.

87. Arranged by Sr. Emily Joseph Daly, C.S.J. and published in this form by the Sisters of St. Joseph of Brentwood, NY in 1955.

88. *Limbo* was originally published in *America* magazine, November 1, 1947.

A SELECTED BIBLIOGRAPHY

(In addition to the Endnotes, the following bibliography will provide further reading on the origins of the spirituality of the Sisters of St. Joseph. Much of the suggested bibliography has been taken from Anne Bernice Hennessey's thesis "The Influence of Ignatian Spirituality in the Primitive Documents of the Sisters of St. Joseph." Sisters of St. Joseph of Orange, CA: 1983).

Aschenbrenner, George A., S.J. "Consciousness Examen." *Review for Religious.* 31 (1972) 14-21.

_____. "A Check on Our Availability: The Examen, *Review for Religious.* 39 (1980) 321-324.

_____. "Consciousness Examen: Becoming God's Heart for the World," *Review for Religious* 47 (1988) 801-810.

_____. "Monasticism of the Heart: The Core of All Christian Lifestyles," *Review for Religious* 49 (1990) 483-498.

Arrupe, Pedro, S.J. "The Trinitarian Charism of the Ignatian Charism." *Centrum Ignatianum Spiritualitatis* 39-40 (1982) 11-69.

Clarke, Thomas, S.J. "The Ignatian Exercises: Contemplation and Discernment." *Review for Religious* 31 (1972): 62-69.

Clancy, Thomas H., S.J. *The Conversational Word of God: A Commentary on the Doctrine of St. Ignatius of Loyola Concerning Spiritual Conversation with Four Early Jesuit Texts.* St. Louis: The Institute of Jesuit Sources, 1978.

Cowan, Marian and Futrell, John, S.J. *The Spiritual Exercises of St. Ignatius Loyola: A Handbook for Directors.* NP: Ministry Training Services, 1981.

De Guibert, Joseph, S.J. *The Jesuits: Their Spiritual Doctrine and Practice.* Translated by Wm. J. Young, S.J. Edited by George E. Ganss, S.J. Chicago: The Institute of Jesuit Sources, 1964.

Egan, Harvey D., S.J. "Karl Rahner: Theologian of the *Spiritual Exercises." Thought*. LXVII/266 (1992) 257-270.

Fleming, David L. S.J. *A Contemporary Reading of the Spiritual Exercises.* St. Louis: Institute of Jesuit Sources, 1976.

Futrell, John S.J. "Communal Discernment." *Supplement to the Way* 14 (1971) 62-70.

Haas, Adolf. "The Foundations of Ignatian Mysticism in Loyola and Manresa." *Centrum Ignatianum Spiritualitatis* 39-40 (1982) 149-196.

Hewitt, William. "The Exercises: A Creative Process." *Supplement to the Way* 42 (1974) 3-16.

"Ignatian Spirituality." *Review for Religious* 50th Anniversary 50/1 (1991).

Ignatius of Loyola. *Constitutions of the Society of Jesus.* Translated with an Introduction and Commentary by George E. Ganss, S.J. St. Louis: Institute of Jesuit Sources, 1970.

Ignatius of Loyola: The Spiritual Exercises and Selected Works. Edited by George E. Ganss, S.J. *et al.* NY & Mahwah, NJ: Paulist Press, 1991.

Ignatius of Loyola: His Personality and Spiritual Heritage. Edited by Friedrich Wulf, S.J. St. Louis: Institute of Jesuit Sources, 1977.

Ivens, Michael. "Ignatius Loyola." in *The Study of Spirituality.* Ed: Cheslyn Jones *et al.* New York & Oxford: Oxford University Press, 1986.

Lochet, Louis. "Apostolic Prayer." in *Finding God in All Things.* Translated by Wm. J. Young, S.J. Chicago, Henry Regnery, 1958, 166-182.

Logue, Sister Maria Kostka. *Sisters of St. Joseph of Philadelphia.* Westminster, MD: Newman Press, 1950.

Mc Carthy, Caritas. "Constitutions for Apostolic Religious." *Supplement to the Way* 14 (1971) 33-45.

_____. "Ignatian Charism in Women's Congregations." *Supplement to the Way* 20 (1973) 10-18.

Maland, David. *Culture and Society in Seventeenth-Century France.* London: Macmillan, 1966.

Meany, Sr. Mary Ignatius, C.S.J. *By Railway or Rainbow.* The Pine Press Brentwood, NY, 1964.

Médaille, Jean-Pierre, S.J. *Constitutions of the Little Congregation of the Sisters of St. Joseph.* Edited by Marius Nepper, S.J. Translated by the Intercongregational Research Team, United States Federation of Sisters of St. Joseph. Erie, PA: Villa Maria College, 1969.

_____. *Maxims of the Little Institute.* Translated by the Intercongregational Research Team, United States Federation of Sisters of St. Joseph. Erie, PA: Villa Maria College, 1975.

_____. *Maxims of Perfection.* Translated by the Intercongregational Research Team, United States Federation of Sisters of St. Joseph. Erie, PA: Villa Maria College, 1979.

_____. *The Reglements and Eucharistic Letter.* Translated by the Intercongregational Research Team, United States Federation of Sisters of St. Joseph. Erie, PA: Villa Maria College, 1973.

Milligan, Mary, R.S.H.M. "Charism and Constitutions." *Supplement to the Way.* 36 (1979) 45-57.

Nepper, Marius, S.J. *Jean Pierre Médaille: Qui Est-ce?* Le Puy-en-Velay: Imp. Jeanne d'Arc, 1963.

_____. *Origins of the Sisters of St. Joseph.* Translated by the Intercongregational Research Team, United States Federation of Sisters of St. Joseph. Erie, PA: Villa Maria College, 1973.

Rahner, Hugo, S.J. *Saint Ignatius of Loyola: Letters to Women.* Translated by Kathleen Pond and S.A.H. Weetman. New York: Herder and Herder, 1960.

_____. *The Spirituality of St. Ignatius of Loyola*. Translated by Francis J. Smith, S.J. Chicago: Loyola University Press, 1953.

Return to the Fountainhead: Addresses at the Tercentenary of the Sisters of St. Joseph, Le Puy, France, 1950. Translated by the Sisters of St. Joseph of Carondelet. Carondelet, MO: By the translators, 1952.

Roccasalvo, Joan L. C.S.J. "The Daily Examen" *Review for Religious,* 46 (March/April 1986): 278-283; reprinted as part of *Best of the Review III: The Christian Ministry of Spiritual Direction* (1988) 312-317.

St. Francis de Sales. *Introduction to the Devout Life*. Newly Translated and edited by John K. Ryan. Garden City, NY: Image Books, 1950.

Schineller, J. Peter, S.J. "The Newer Approaches to Christology and Their Use in the Spiritual Exercises." *Studies in the Spirituality of Jesuits* XII (1980).

Singles, Sister Dona. *Jean Pierre Médaille's Little Design*. Nazareth, MI: Sisters of St. Joseph, 1973.

Stanley, David M., S.J. "Contemplation of the Gospels, Ignatius Loyola and the Contemporary Christian." *Theological Studies* 29 (1968) 417-443.

_____. "The Eucharistic Letter: Heart of the Spirituality of Jean Pierre Médaille, S.J." Paper presented to the Sisters of St. Joseph of Orange, CA: October 1979.

_____. *A Modern Scriptural Approach to the Spiritual Exercises*. St. Louis: Institute of Jesuit Sources, 1971.

Toner, Jules, S.J. "A Method for Communal Discernment." *Studies in the Spirituality of Jesuits* III (1971).

Whelan, Joseph P. S.J. "Jesuit Apostolic Prayer." *Supplement to The Way*. 19 (1973) 13-21.

110

(The following material is located in the Archives of the C/SSJ Federation.)

Aucoin, Sr. Jane. "Spirit and Spirituality of the Sisters of St. Joseph." Newton, MA. 1974.

Berry, Sr. Margaret. "Charism, the Movement toward Unity." La Grange, IL: 1984. (Cassette tape)

Clarke, Thomas, S.J. "Key to Conversion: the Humble Jesus." St. Paul, MN: 1973.

_____. "Jesus, the Center of Reconciliation in a Rapidly Changing World." St. Paul, MN: 1973.

Cowan, Sr. Marian. "Apostolic Spirituality for Sisters of St. Joseph." Orange, CA: 1988. (Cassette tape)

Dooley, Sr. Mary. "Rooted in Christ Jesus." Wichita, KS: 1979. (Cassette tape)

Flynn, Sr. Monica. "Charism--the Sisters of St. Joseph of Wheeling." Wheeling, WV: 1984.

Harkins, Sr. Julie. "Spirit and Spirituality of the Congregation." Boston, MA: 1975. (Cassette tape)

Hennessey, Sr. Anne Bernice, C.S.J. "The Influence of Ignatian Spirituality in the Primitive Documents of the Sisters of St. Joseph." Sisters of St. Joseph of Orange, CA: 1983.

Keating, Sr. Kathleen. "Adapting Our Charism for the Signs of the Times." Holyoke, MA: 1984. (Cassette tape)

Mc Carthy, Sr. Kathleen. "The Consensus Statement: Charism and Early History of the Sisters of St. Joseph." Los Angeles, CA: 1983. (Cassette tape)

Marshall, Sr. Ann. "Mission and Charism." Toronto, 1985. (Cassette tape)

Médaille Committee of the Sisters of St. Joseph of Bourg. "The Spirituality of Rev. Jean Pierre Médaille, S.J., Founder of the Sisters of St. Joseph. New Orleans, LA: 1967.

Moslander, Sr. Bette. "Charism." Nazareth, MI 1978.

_____. "Culture and Charism." Nazareth, MI: 1978.

_____. "Charism of the Congregation of Sisters of St. Joseph." Chestnut Hill, MA: 1982.

_____. "Charism Lived out into the Future. 1988.

_____. "Rooted in Christ Jesus." Wichita, 79. (Cassette tapes)